access to history

themes

D1313412

THE
of DEMOCRACY in
BRITAIN

Annette Mayer

& Stoughton

A MEMBER OF THE HODDER HEADLINE GROUP

Acknowledgements

The publishers would like to thank the following for permission to reproduce material in this volume: Allen & Unwin Ltd for an extract from *The Age of Lord George* by Kenneth O. Morgan (1971); J.M. Dent & Son for an extract from *Reflections on the French Revolution and Other Essays* by Edmund Burke (1940); Everyman for an extract from *The Rights of Man* by Thomas Paine, edited by Tony Benn (1993); Faber and Faber for an extract from *The Growth of Philosophic Radicalism* by Elie Halevy (1952); Leicester University Press for an extract from *Chartism - a new organisation of the People* by W. Lovett and J. Collins (1969); Macmillan Press Ltd for an extract from 'Some Practices and Problems of Chartist Democracy', by Eileen Yeo in *The Chartist Experience: Studies in Working-Class Radicalism and Cultures, 1830-60* edited by D. Thompson and James Epstein (1982); Macmillan Publishers Ltd for an extract from *Democracy and the Organization of Political Parties* by M. Ostrogorski (1902); James Nisbett & Co for an extract from *Imperialism: A Study* by J.A. Hobson (1902); Oxford University Press for an extract from John Stuart Mill, *On Liberty and Other Essays* edited by John Gray (1998); Penguin Books Ltd for an extract by Benjamin Disraeli, 24 June 1872 from *The Penguin Book of Historic Speeches* edited by Brian Macarthur (1996); The *Sun* for an extract from The *Sun*, 9 April 1992; Routledge for an extract from *Essays on Government, Jurisprudence, Liberty of the Press and Law of Nations* by James Mill (1992) and for an extract from *Speeches of Lord Randolph Churchill* edited by H.W. Lucy (1885); Virago Press for an extract from *The Suffrage Movement* by E.S. Pankhurst (1977).

The publishers would like to thank the following for permission to reproduce copyright illustrations in this volume: Pages 19, 40, 56, 101, 108 and 109 reproduced courtesy of the Bodleian Library, Oxford; page 43 'The National Convention' from *History of the Chartist Movement 1837-1854* by RG Gammage (1894) reproduced courtesy of the British Library.

Every effort has been made to trace and acknowledge ownership of copyright. The publishers will be glad to make any suitable arrangements with copyright holders whom it has not been possible to contact.

British Library Cataloguing in Publication Data
A catalogue for this title is available from the British Library

ISBN 0 340 69792 X

First published 1999

Impression number	10	9	8	7	6	5	4	3
Year			2004	2003	2002			

The cover shows Palmerston addressing the Commons painted by John Phillip (1863) reproduced courtesy of the Bridgeman Art Library, London.

Typeset by Sempringham publishing services, Bedford.
Printed in Great Britain for Hodder & Stoughton Educational,
a division of Hodder Headline Plc, 338 Euston Road, London NW1 3BH
by The Bath Press, Bath

Contents

Preface

The original *Access to History* series was conceived as a collection of sets of books covering popular chronological periods in British history, such as 'the Tudors' and 'the nineteenth century', together with the histories of other countries, such as France, Germany, Russia and the USA. This arrangement complemented the way in which early-modern and modern history has traditionally been taught in sixth forms, colleges and universities. In recent years, however, other ways of dividing up the past have become increasingly popular. In particular, there has been a greater emphasis on studying relatively brief periods in considerable detail and on comparing similar historical phenomena in different countries. These developments have generated a demand for appropriate learning materials, and, in response, two new 'strands' are being added to the main series - *In Depth* and *Themes*. The new volumes build directly on the features that have made *Access to History* so popular.

To the general reader

Although *Access* books have been specifically designed to meet the needs of examination students, these volumes also have much to offer the general reader. *Access* authors are committed to the belief that good history must not only be accurate, up-to-date and scholarly, but also clearly and attractively written. The main body of the text (excluding the 'Study Guides') should, therefore, form a readable and engaging survey of a topic. Moreover, each author has aimed not merely to provide as clear an explanation as possible of what happened in the past but also to stimulate readers and to challenge them into thinking for themselves about the past and its significance. Thus, although no prior knowledge is expected from the reader, he or she is treated as an intelligent and thinking person throughout. The author tends to share ideas and explore possibilities, instead of delivering so-called 'historical truths' from on high.

To the student reader

It is intended that *Access* books should be used by students studying history at a higher level. Its volumes are all designed to be working texts, which should be reasonably clear on a first reading but which will benefit from re-reading and close study. To be an effective and successful student, you need to budget your time wisely. Hence you should think carefully about how important the material in a particular book is for you. If you simply need to acquire a general grasp of a topic, the following approach will probably be effective:

I. Read Chapter 1, which should give you an overview of the whole book, and think about its contents.

2. Skim through Chapter 2, paying particular attention to the opening section and to the headings and sub-headings. Decide if you need to read the whole chapter.
3. If you do, read the chapter, stopping at the end of every sub-division of the text to make notes.
4. Repeat stage 2 (and stage 3 where appropriate) for the other chapters.

If, however, your course - and your particular approach to it - demands a detailed knowledge of the contents of the book, you will need to be correspondingly more thorough. There is no perfect way of studying, and it is particularly worthwhile experimenting with different styles of note-making to find the one that best suits you. Nevertheless, the following plan of action is worth trying:

1. Read a whole chapter quickly, preferably at one sitting. Avoid the temptation - which may be very great - to make notes at this stage.
2. Study the flow diagram at the end of the chapter, ensuring that you understand the general 'shape' of what you have read.
3. Re-read the chapter more slowly, this time taking notes. You may well be amazed at how much more intelligible and straightforward the material seems on a second reading - and your notes will be correspondingly more useful to you when you have to write an essay or revise for an exam. In the long run, reading a chapter twice can, in fact, often save time. Be sure to make your notes in a clear, orderly fashion, and spread them out so that, if necessary, you can later add extra information.
4. Read the advice on essay questions, and do tackle the specimen titles. (Remember that if learning is to be effective, it must be active. No one - alas - has yet devised any substitute for real effort. It is up to you to make up your own mind on the key issues in any topic.)
5. Attempt the source-based questions. The guidance on tackling these exercises, which is generally given at least once in a book, is well worth reading and thinking about.

When you have finished the main chapters, go through the 'Further Reading' section. Remember that no single book can ever do more than introduce a topic, and it is to be hoped that - time permitting - you will want to read more widely. If *Access* books help you to discover just how diverse and fascinating the human past can be, the series will have succeeded in its aim - and you will experience that enthusiasm for the subject which, along with efficient learning, is the hallmark of all the best students.

Robert Pearce

1 The Concept of Democracy in Britain

In his book entitled *Politics*, Aristotle wrote, 'Man is by nature a political animal'.[1] Since ancient times, man has sought to protect himself, his family, his community and his country by means of law and order. A civilised society avoids chaos by establishing a method of government that will provide appropriate laws and security. The nation state survives because its people and its leaders are political animals. Their personal interests have a communal, or political, dimension which becomes intrinsically linked with the interests of the wider community.

Today, as we survey the political systems of the modern world, we see a range of political ideas determining the nature of government. Some countries are still subjected to a military-style leadership, where power is associated with the army. Elsewhere, a civilian government rules but political power rests in the hands of one party. Political opposition is suppressed. In Britain, as in many other countries, we pride ourselves on upholding the principle of democratic government.

It is a fragile principle which, even in the twentieth century, has been frequently challenged. Greece, once the cradle of democracy, was ruled by the military between 1967 and 1974. For modern Spain, the principle is still a recent phenomenon; before 1975, the country was ruled for 36 years by the fascist dictator General Franco. The most serious threats to the survival of democracy in this century were undoubtedly the two World Wars. In a speech to the American Congress on 2 April 1917, President Woodrow Wilson said, 'The world must be made safe for democracy'. Four days later, America decided that she could no longer maintain her position of neutrality and declared war on Germany. During the Second World War, Churchill defined Britain's policy as one in which we were waging 'war against a monstrous tyranny, never surpassed in the dark, lamentable catalogue of human crime'.[2] Millions of lives were lost in order to restore and preserve democracy.

1 Modern Democratic Britain

What, therefore, is considered to be so precious about democracy? Why do we value it so highly, to the extent that we will condemn and criticise all undemocratic governments? What are the attributes of democracy that have become so essential to uphold?

a) The Electoral Process

In Britain, as in many other countries, we claim to be democratic because a government is freely elected by popular vote. Every man and woman aged 18 or over is eligible to vote, provided that they are a British subject and their name appears on the electoral register. The age limit of 18 does not embody an important democratic principle but is rather a reflection of the arbitrary decisions which are sometimes necessary when establishing a democracy. The only exceptions to this right are members of the House of Lords, including the royal family, and those who are either mentally incapacitated or in prison. The right to vote by all adults is known as universal suffrage and is regarded as an intrinsic element of any democratic system. Not all countries, therefore, have full democracy because they may impose some restrictions on the criteria for granting the vote, or franchise.

Today there are few barriers to becoming a Member of Parliament (MP). Anyone entitled to vote may stand, apart from bankrupts, clergy and holders of certain public offices. A deposit of £500 is required which is forfeited if the candidate gains less than five per cent of the votes. Thus the electorate can select their MPs from a range of candidates who not only represent various political parties, but also different religious and ethnic origins. The wide diversity of backgrounds - gender, religion and race - of MPs who were successfully elected in the May 1997 general election reflected more than any previous election the multi-faceted nature of modern Britain.

In each constituency, the system of first-past-the-post operates, whereby the successful candidate is the one who gains the most votes. Most candidates belong to one or other of the main political parties - Conservative or Labour - although the Liberal Democrats are a significant third party. The political party commanding the highest number of MPs forms the government, as long as they have a majority over all other parties in the House of Commons. Failure to achieve this majority necessitates negotiations with smaller, minority parties for their support. Parliament is, therefore, directly elected by the people. If the government proves unsatisfactory, it can be dismissed from office by popular vote, just as Churchill was defeated in 1945. This is a fundamental principle of representative democracy.

b) Parliament

In Britain, the seat of democracy is Parliament, which consists of the Queen, the House of Lords and the House of Commons. Over the last two centuries the monarch's executive role has gradually diminished so that, as Head of State, the Queen's role is now largely symbolic and ceremonial. She sanctions the decisions of her government, ratifying Acts of Parliament, but she does not initiate policy. She reigns but she does not rule. In theory, the monarch appoints the prime minister and government ministers. In practice, it is the leader who commands a majority in the House of Commons who automatically becomes prime minister and he or she will nominate the members of the

Cabinet. Thus we have a constitutional monarchy whose functions have been severely restricted over the last 200 years.

Likewise, the powers exerted by the House of Lords have been reduced so that legislation can only be delayed by the Upper House. It is in the House of Commons, where freely elected representatives assemble, that executive government resides. Here legislation is introduced, discussed and passes onto the statute books. Although a government with a considerable majority can usually be confident that its proposed laws will be passed, an important aspect of a democratic state is that such laws can be freely debated and amended by the different political parties in the Commons. It was Hitler's ban on all other political parties other than the Nazis in 1933 which marked the abrupt end to democracy in Germany.

c) The Constitution

One notable feature of democracy in Britain is that it is sustained by an unwritten constitution. The constitution is the system of laws which determines the way the country is governed and which establishes the relationship between the people and their representatives. Unlike America where the rules of government are incorporated within a written constitution, Britain has a constitution which has evolved over centuries. No single document contains the constitution: rather it is a mixture of written laws, i.e. Acts of Parliament, judicial decisions, conventions and traditions which have come to be regarded as accepted practice. For example, before 1911 there was an unwritten agreement between the House of Lords and the House of Commons that the former would not veto any financial bill presented by the government. When the House of Lords rejected Lloyd George's budget in 1909, a constitutional crisis ensued which culminated in the Parliament Act of 1911, restricting the Lords' right of veto.

d) Features of Democracy

But there are other features which help to constitute a democracy. Free elections cannot proceed without freedom of speech. How else could one political party expound their ideas unless they were permitted to proclaim the merits of their own policies and also reveal the alleged weaknesses of their opponents' policies? The people likewise must be free to criticise their representatives without fear of retaliation. Naturally there are laws to protect individuals, such as from libel or racially discriminatory remarks; nevertheless, the right to express openly differing political views is seen as an inherent aspect of democracy. Otherwise democracy may be merely a facade.

Correlated with freedom of speech is the need for a free press and media. Joseph Goebbels, as Hitler's Minister for Propaganda and

National Enlightenment, successfully manipulated the thoughts of the German population during the 1930s and 1940s through newspapers, literature and the media. The evil consequences of his propaganda illustrated all too graphically the dangers of censorship and the suppression of free speech. The fact that the British government respects the independence of the press and television is a further indication that Britain upholds the principles of democracy.

Religious and racial toleration constitute another cornerstone of democracy in Britain. In a country which is now distinctly multi-cultural, discrimination against any minority group is greatly to be abhorred. It can be argued, therefore, that only in a genuine democracy can the rights of minorities be respected. In a democracy it is seen as the duty of the majority to protect those in a minority.

It is widely regarded that our parliamentary system of government is one to be safeguarded. The combined role of monarchy, parliament and the judiciary has resulted in what is described as a liberal democracy, one which many people consider to be unique. At one time Britons were convinced that this was the best of all possible systems, and a model for the rest of the world. Now we tend to be a little more self-critical. But this is a good thing, for democracy needs aware and critical citizens. The extent to which we should reappraise and reform our democratic system will be a question to explore at the conclusion of this book.

2 The Historical Development of Democracy

a) Simple Democracy

The political debate about the future of democracy in Britain is not just a modern phenomenon. The concept of democracy has been discussed, practised and abused for hundreds of centuries. 'Democracy' derives from the Greek words *demos*, 'the people', and *kratein*, 'to rule'. Ancient Greece consisted of a number of city states, of which Athens was one of the greatest. In the fifth century BC all citizens native to Athens could both vote and speak in a government assembly, with the exception of women and slaves. This system of 'direct democracy' was feasible because Athens was a small community. Each individual could be involved, gathering collectively in the public squares where decisions on government matters - laws and foreign affairs - were made. Magistrates were expected to account publicly for their decisions. What signified in Ancient Athens was the authority of the community as a whole. This took precedent over the liberty of the individual. The freedom of the individual to make private decisions, such as choosing a religion, was restricted on the grounds that the interests of society were paramount.

This simple form of democracy had its drawbacks. Whilst subsequent political thinkers praised the concept of direct political involvement, it was recognised that this would be impractical in larger communities. How could societies with populations of thousands manage the logistical problem of direct participation? It was, therefore, the more modern concept of democracy, that of a *representative* democracy, which influenced the evolution of democratic government in Britain.

b) Representative Government versus Absolute Monarchy

Britain has possessed a parliament since the thirteenth century, although its initial role was essentially to enact the directives of the monarch who could summon Parliament as and when desired. Henry VII held only one Parliament during the last 12 years of his reign. Under Henry VIII and Elizabeth I, Parliament assumed a more critical role - Henry VIII used Parliament to define the new relationship between Church and State - but it was not until the reign of Charles I that the precise function of Parliament came under close scrutiny. In 1629, angered by MPs' refusal to sanction certain policies, Charles I dismissed Parliament and did not recall it for 11 years. Yet whereas Charles's predecessors had traditionally convened or dispensed with Parliament at will, his acts were seen by the Commons as too arbitrary. Many MPs now considered it customary for them to be consulted regularly as representatives of the people. If a monarch sought to combine the role of legislator, judge and jury, he stood in danger of becoming an absolute monarch. In these circumstances, the people would have no redress against loss of civil liberties, nor could Parliament offer the people protection. The ensuing conflict between Charles and his Parliament reflected the determination of MPs not to be dictated to by the whims of one man.

The Civil War and subsequent events heralded a period of instability in British politics. John Locke (1632-1704) was a leading political theorist and philosopher whose arguments reiterated many contemporary views regarding the need for constitutional limits on the Crown. His *Two Treatises* revealed his opposition to tyranny and arbitrary government. Locke disputed the idea that the monarch's political authority was derived from God - the concept known as Divine Right - because it could lead to absolute monarchy which, he asserted, was 'inconsistent with civil society, and so can be no form of civil government at all'.[3] In Locke's view, sovereignty resided in the people and government depended upon their direct consent. A government's role was to protect the rights and liberties of the people, but if the governors failed to rule according to the laws then they would forfeit the people's trust. The people possessed the right to choose an alternative government.

Locke's views on government were particularly pertinent because their publication came just as Britain was seeking to check yet again the dangers of abuse of power by the monarch. The crisis in question was the determination of James II to reinstate the Roman Catholic succession to the throne in 1687. These actions were viewed as autocratic and unconstitutional and resulted in his exile to France in 1688. His exile was instigated by Parliament, whose Members then invited the Protestant William of Orange to be James's successor. The important point to note is that Parliament successfully exercised its authority both over the outgoing and incoming monarchs. In the case of the latter, Parliament determined the conditions under which William accepted the Crown.

c) The Revolution Settlement and the Bill of Rights

These conditions took the form of the Revolution Settlement of 1688 and the Bill of Rights of 1689. The Revolution Settlement secured the supremacy of Parliament whilst the Bill of Rights abolished the prerogative of the King to rule by decree, compelling him to consult with Parliament. The monarch still retained the right to choose his own ministers and to summon or dissolve Parliament, but now he could only raise taxes with Parliament's annual consent. Finally, the Protestant succession was secured, prohibiting any Roman Catholic or anyone married to a Roman Catholic from becoming monarch. These agreements guaranteed that the authority of Parliament could not be undermined.

3 The Nature of Government in the Eighteenth Century

In subsequent years, political debate, inspired by the more liberal attitudes of the European Enlightenment, was to focus on the relationship between Parliament and the people and on the structure of representative government. As will be seen in Chapter 2, much of the impetus for change developed at the end of the eighteenth century, when various external and internal events challenged the *status quo*. First, it is necessary to understand the precise nature of government in the eighteenth century. What were the attributes of government which today would seem so unfamiliar and to what extent were these features undemocratic? Only then can the extent to which radical change took place over the next 200 years be appreciated.

a) The Problems of the Franchise and Representation

Whereas today every adult over the age of 18 can vote, in 1780 the franchise was very restricted. In England and Wales, about one in eight men could vote, the figure being lower in Scotland and Ireland. This gave a total electorate of around 214,000 out of a population of approximately eight million. The right to vote depended very much on one's locality because there was no uniform franchise. In the counties, all freeholders, i.e. those people whose property had a rateable value of more than 40 shillings (£2) a year, possessed the franchise. In the boroughs, a number of qualifying systems prevailed, ranging from burgage boroughs, where the landlord or ancient burgage tenant had the vote, to corporation boroughs, where corporation members, usually shopkeepers and business men, were entitled to the suffrage. Whilst gentry, clergy, professionals, tradesmen, craftsmen, retailers and even some unskilled workers might qualify for the vote, nationwide the system was inconsistent. One factor did remain constant - with few exceptions, the voter had to possess property. This requirement automatically excluded large sections of the population from the electoral system and, without exception, it debarred all women from voting.

This variation in the franchise was aggravated by geography. Today, the Boundary Commission reassesses population distribution every ten years in order to ensure that constituencies are neither under nor over-populated. Constituency boundaries are redrawn accordingly. In the eighteenth century, however, MPs were far from being the representatives of their constituents. First, as indicated above, only a certain percentage of their constituents could vote. Secondly, the ratio of MPs to population fluctuated wildly. Some ancient boroughs were totally depopulated yet still returned two MPs. Dunwich, on the Suffolk coast, had virtually collapsed into the North Sea yet its remaining 32 electors sent two representatives to Parliament. Twenty-two boroughs had under 300 voters each. In contrast, the expanding industrial towns of the north such as Manchester and Leeds had no MPs at all. The effects of urbanisation and the need for representation had yet to be recognised by Parliament. Finally, the bias towards the south of England was very strong. A third of England's MPs were concentrated in the six English counties bordering the south coast. What is clear is that parliamentary government was far from being even remotely representative of the people. This factor, combined with the extensive influence exerted by a small group of people, helped to constitute the very undemocratic nature of eighteenth-century government.

b) The Influence of Patronage

i) The Road to the House of Commons

Another prominent feature of eighteenth-century government was the narrow background of MPs. As MPs were unpaid, their income had to be derived from other sources; hence the majority came from landowning families. In many cases, the eldest son of a peer would sit in the House of Lords, whilst his younger brothers sought a career in the House of Commons. Following the general election of 1784, some 55 per cent of MPs had landed connections. The Commons resembled a big aristocratic club where membership depended on birth and acquaintance.

Today, potential parliamentary candidates go through a rigorous selection procedure before being adopted to represent their political party. An interviewing panel will pose questions on party policy, as well as testing the candidate's suitability to represent the interests of his or her constituents. Once appointed, candidates have to manage a campaign which not only publicises the manifesto commitments of their own party, but also attacks the ideas of the opponents. Each constituency is contested, sometimes by as many as ten candidates.

This is far removed from the election practices of the eighteenth century. The influence of the aristocracy was pervasive. Great landowners dictated the composition of the Commons by dispensing patronage. As the owner of a large estate, a peer or baronet could nominate the candidate for the parliamentary constituency covered by his land. It was in his remit to bestow this favour on whomever he chose, frequently a close relative of his family. His subsequent support for the candidate would usually guarantee that person's election to the Commons, although in return the candidate had to demonstrate his loyalty by voting according to the wishes of his patron. The alternative to acquiring a seat through patronage was to buy a seat. Once again, this narrowed the field of candidates to those with considerable incomes. One might have avoided the stigma of being in the pocket of a great landlord but one still needed perhaps £10,000 (the equivalent of over £1 million today) to acquire independence.

Contested elections were rare. To mount a successful challenge in a seat controlled by a landlord would probably result in financial ruin because election expenses would become exorbitant. Few men could compete with the patronage of a powerful landlord such as the Duke of Bedford or the Earl of Lonsdale, whose control of the borough of Carlisle enabled him to direct the votes of 14,000 miners.

Corruption was, therefore, an inescapable fact of life in the eighteenth century. It meant that the opportunity to pursue a career in politics was closed to all but a small group of wealthy aristocrats. Effectively, Britain was ruled by an aristocratic oligarchy. An oligarchy was a form of government where power was exercised by the few with the express purpose of upholding their self-interest.

ii) Parliament

The effects of patronage inside Parliament were as invasive as they were outside. Consequently, the familiar pattern of twentieth-century party politics was far less distinct in the eighteenth century. Whereas politicians today adhere to the politics of their party - Conservative, Labour or Liberal Democrat - and are disciplined by their party if they transgress from the party line, eighteenth-century politicians frequently displayed a stronger allegiance to a political family than to a party. This was a direct result of the effect of patronage on politics.

An influential political patron commanded loyalty and hence implemented substantial control over the voting behaviour of his nominees. Although two parties - the Whigs and the Tories - had developed during the course of the eighteenth century, MPs were still inclined to vote independently of their party.

The influence of political families penetrated all levels of government. At the top of the hierarchical system of patronage was the monarch, still able to choose his ministers. Beneath him, the powerful political landowners awarded high-ranking posts to people known and personally recommended to them. Status and background were far more likely to be considered than a candidate's intellectual merits. The only group of MPs to be immune from influence were the Independent members who numbered about 200 in 1784. They had been elected without being dependent on a patron and were in most cases landowners in their own right.

Factional interests dominated eighteenth-century government right up to 1784. Control of the Commons was a complex arrangement with political agreements frequently being negotiated. Yet if any party could claim to dominate proceedings it was the Whigs, especially after 1714. The Tories had suffered because of their association with the disastrous efforts to engineer a pro-Catholic Stuart revival in 1714. This embarrassing event led to their forming the Opposition. The Whigs, on the other hand, now enjoyed a period of hegemony, during which neither George I nor George II sought to limit their authority. This was abruptly terminated when, in 1784, George III installed William Pitt as Prime Minister. Unlike his predecessors, George III was not prepared to play a passive role in politics and insisted that he, not the politicians, should select the Prime Minister and members of the Cabinet.

This particular crisis had important implications for future ideas on democracy. It drew MPs' attention to the fact that the monarch could exert considerable political influence. Given that these events occurred soon after Britain's constitutional dispute with her American colonies and coincided with the French Revolution, it illustrated the need to re-examine the balance of power between monarch and House of Commons. For Parliament, therefore, the overriding concern was how to impose limits on the influence of the Crown.

4 The Growth of Democracy

The end of the eighteenth century in British politics can be considered as a watershed in terms of constitutional history. Over the next 200 years, far-reaching changes occurred. During that period, Britain evolved from being ruled by an aristocratic oligarchy, selected on the basis of a very limited franchise and representing sectional interests, to possessing a more comprehensive and representative government, chosen by universal suffrage. How did this radical change take place?

The challenges to the parliamentary system were wide-ranging. The 1780s and 1790s were turbulent decades as the country responded to the impact of revolutions in America and France. Fears that the dominance of the aristocratic elite would be undermined influenced government reaction to these external events. Their long-term effect was considerable. Radical reformers were inspired by fresh ideas as issues of equality, liberty and the injustices of taxation gained support. Extensive political debate fuelled interest in reform to the extent that governments could not resist demands for political change forever.

The relationship between the government and its people was dramatically affected by socio-economic developments. The Industrial Revolution and the consequent expansion of both the middle class and an urban working class could not fail to undermine the monopoly of power enjoyed by the aristocracy. Once the government responded to these factors, in terms of granting both political and economic reforms, Britain started to turn away from the limited parliamentary government of the eighteenth century.

During the nineteenth century, it is possible to discern the evolution of a more popular form of politics. This was manifested in several ways. First, there was the gradual expansion of the franchise, in 1832, 1867 and 1884. Secondly, political parties themselves perceived the need to be more democratic. By the 1860s, the era of the mass voter was becoming more of a reality and potential supporters had to be wooed. Party organisation was reformed in order to win the minds of the new electorate. Thirdly, it was also appreciated that the public was becoming more politically conscious. They were no longer so deferential to their superiors, and hence politicians had to be more accountable to and representative of their constituents' interests. Finally, by the end of the nineteenth century, the issues of working-class politics and the female franchise had become more prominent.

Yet in contrast to many European countries, Britain managed to embrace these features of a democratic state without violent upheaval. Britain's transformation to a modern, representative democracy was, therefore, a distinctly British experience, one which ensured stability as well as continuity with the past.

References

1 Aristotle, *The Politics*, Book 1, 1253a2-3 (Oxford University Press, 1995), p.10.
2 *Hansard's Parliamentary Debates*, 5th Series, vol.360, 13 May 1940, col.1502.
3 John Locke, 'Second Treatise of Government', II, sec.90, in Steven M. Cahn, *Classics of Modern Theory* (Oxford University Press, 1997), p.243.

Summary Diagram
The Concept of Democracy in Britain

The Age of Oligarchy - Britain in the Eighteenth Century	The Age of Democracy - Britain in the Twentieth Century
rule of aristocracy	→ popular government
limited franchise	→ universal suffrage
under-representation	→ equal-sized constituencies
no secret ballot	→ secret ballot
unpaid MPs	→ paid MPs
politically involved monarch	→ constitutional monarchy
corruption, patronage	→ reformed electoral practices
little party loyalty	→ party politics
unwritten constitution	→ unwritten constitution

2 External and Internal Challenges, 1780-1868

At the end of the eighteenth century the oligarchical system of government in Britain (see page 8) came under attack from several different directions. The Revolution Settlement of 1688 had addressed the key issues concerning the abuse of power by the monarchy and had successfully established Parliament's role in providing the necessary checks and balances to the monarchy. But it was clear by the end of the eighteenth century that this was not enough: the nation's interests were not being effectively represented by the ruling classes (see pages 7-9).

Several challenges to the system of government emerged between 1780 and 1868 which in the long term influenced the development of democracy in Britain. The first came from the middle classes who increasingly questioned the rights and privileges of the aristocracy. Until 1815 this multi-layered group of the middle ranks of society, ranging from merchants and bankers to clergymen and small farmers, had broadly accepted that political power should reside in the hands of the great landowners. For centuries, the aristocracy had enjoyed a monopoly of power, claiming their authority from a general acceptance that property and patronage provided a legitimate basis for government. In part, acceptance of the aristocracy reflected the fact that it did not close its ranks to newcomers. Society was mobile, with members of the middling classes able to enrich themselves and acquire both property and titles. Conversely, younger members of landed families moved downwards in order to embark on careers in commerce and industry. As a consequence, these two sections of society, aristocracy and middle classes, maintained a form of social equilibrium in which each was able to respect and accommodate the other.

But as the size and wealth of the middle classes increased, this 'dynamic social equilibrium'[1] which characterised pre-industrial English society came under threat. The fact that government and authority were derived so directly from the ownership of property and the distribution of patronage proved increasingly irksome to a group of people who found their growing economic status unmatched by political recognition. As the economic benefits of the commercial and industrial revolution emerged, these groups questioned the aristocracy's monopoly of power. Economic growth therefore led to mounting hostility between the upper and middle groups of society.

The second key influence on the changing structure of government in Britain came from the political ideas inspired by the revolutions in America and France. The American bid for independence from Britain from 1776 raised important questions about the relationship between governors and their subjects. These prompted similar debates in Britain, encouraging British political reformers to seek improvements in the British system of representation. With the onset of revolution in France in 1789 these ideas gained further momentum.

Several key political writers laid the foundations for this debate. Thomas Paine was inspired by events in America, and become a central figure within the American independence movement. Shortly thereafter the French Revolution, with its revolutionary ideas of *equalité, fraternité et liberté*, became the beacon of democracy. Paine's involvement in both revolutions provided him with the credentials to become a leading radical thinker in Britain. Edmund Burke also influenced reformers, encouraging those who were alienated by the excesses of the French Revolution to articulate a more moderate challenge to oligarchical government. Jeremy Bentham and James Mill were two further writers whose ideas on representation seemed to reflect aptly the demands and desires of the expanding capitalist middle class and who both successfully highlighted the inadequacies of the existing parliamentary system. By the time government was ready to admit not just the middle classes to the franchise but also the urban working class, the writings of J.S. Mill and Walter Bagehot provided an appropriate framework for the extension of the franchise, albeit according to criteria which still accepted property as the basis for political rights. Thus by 1868, the middle class had emerged as a power group whose dominance in politics provided a very distinctive identity to the subsequent form of democracy in Britain.

1 The Industrial Revolution

In 1832, the middle classes, followed by the urban working classes in 1867, were successful in gaining the franchise. Their achievements, however, cannot be simply attributed to the actions of an enlightened ruling elite. (See page 14 for details of the 1832 and 1867 Reform Acts.) The move to greater democracy was far more complex, involving the interaction of several different factors, of which the Industrial Revolution was probably the single most important.

The period of the Industrial Revolution was characterised by a combination of population growth, modernisation of the means of production in both industry and agriculture, expansion of manufacturing output and a transformation in transport. The population expanded by approximately 75 per cent between 1801 and 1851. This caused an increased demand for food which was met by more efficient crop production, scientific breeding of livestock and further enclosure of land. Even so, as a percentage of national income, agriculture (together with fisheries and forestry) fell from 32.5 per cent in 1801 to 20.3 per cent in 1851.

The reason for this decrease was that manufacturing grew even more rapidly during the same period, from 23.4 per cent to 34.3 per cent of national income, clear proof that Britain was establishing herself as a leading producer of manufactured goods. The explanation for the country's success lay not so much in the growth of factories - the majority of workers in 1830 were still employed in workshops with fewer than 30 employees - but in the proliferation of scientific ideas and the burst of entrepreneurial enthusiasm which encouraged industrial expansion. For example, the introduction of steam had a major impact on both production and transport, helping to transform the British economy.

Political Reform 1832-67

The 1832 Reform Act
a) Qualifications for the Vote.
The County Franchise:
retained the old 40 shilling freehold qualification and extended the franchise to £10 copyholders and tenants leasing or renting land worth £50 per annum.
The Borough Franchise:
granted a uniform franchise to all adult males owning or renting property worth £10 per annum, as long as they had not received poor relief during the previous year. Members of pre-1832 categories of voters, who were now disqualified, retained their vote for their lifetime under certain conditions.

b) Redistribution of Seats
56 English boroughs with populations of less than 2,000 were disenfranchised; 30 boroughs with populations between 2,000 and 4,000 lost one of their two MPs; 22 new boroughs were created with two MPs and 20 with one MP.
In total, 143 seats were redistributed.

The Second Reform Act, 1867
a) Qualifications for the Vote
The County Franchise:
extended the vote to all owners or leaseholders of property worth £5 per annum, to £12 occupiers and those owning or renting land with a rateable value of £12 per annum.
The Borough Franchise:
granted to all male householders and lodgers paying £10 rent per annum, provided they had been resident for one year.
b) Redistribution of Seats
52 seats were redistributed, including 25 to the counties, 20 to new boroughs, 6 boroughs received an additional MP and London University gained a seat.

With the Industrial Revolution came new expectations. Members of the middle to upper classes, who could not maintain their economic well-being through the possession of land, turned to enterprise to gain status and wealth. The middle classes were ideally placed to take advantage of the economic boom associated with the Industrial Revolution. Men such as Josiah Wedgewood, a self-educated potter, and Richard Arkwright, the creator of the Water Frame and one of the key architects of the factory system, exemplified the spirit of this new age. In the latter years of the eighteenth century, their factories provided a model for future capitalist developments. With the growth of the factory system, however, it became more difficult to maintain the caring face of industrialisation which they had initiated. Factories had to be managed, workers controlled and disciplined. The result was the emergence of the factory manager who acted to suppress the freedoms of employees and ensure maximum profits for the owners of capital. The gap between the classes widened, creating a more class-conscious society, one in which different income groups would seek more actively to pursue their own individual interests.

Increased wealth shifted the attitudes and aspirations of the middle classes. They perceived themselves as important contributors to the economy, a view endorsed by the writer Adam Smith. In his *Wealth of Nations* (1776), Smith advocated the concept of *laissez-faire*, whereby free competition promoted economic well-being. There should be minimal regulation by government to allow owners of capital to embark on capitalist enterprises without restraints. Wage levels were determined by employer and employee, and in turn were influenced by the demand for goods and the availability of labour. In these conditions of the free market, the self-made man, the entrepreneur, would flourish, taking advantage of the emerging new ideas and inventions. Such men were able to claim their place in society on the basis of their contribution to economic growth and national prosperity.

This view contrasted sharply with that of eighteenth-century Britain. The philosophy of efficiency and economy, applied to social and government policies, now replaced patronage and benevolent care. The administration of the Poor Law was just one illustration of how attitudes towards the lower classes were changing. The Elizabethan Poor Laws were viewed as inappropriate in a developing industrial society: the concept that the wealthy should support and provide for the poor contradicted the *laissez-faire* views of Smith or the economic analysis of Thomas Malthus (*Essay on the Principle of Population*, 1798), who argued that subsistence obstructed free competition. As a result, the rights of protection were gradually removed, culminating in a national system designed to deter the poor from being a financial burden. The Poor Law Amendment Act of 1834, with its dreaded workhouses, epitomised the way the benevolent care of the poor had been replaced by the principle of efficiency.

The introduction of the Combination Acts in 1799 and 1800 was yet further evidence of society being governed by free market forces. They prevented workers from establishing combinations or unions in their individual trades to protect their rights and allowed employers greater flexibility in fixing terms of employment. Thus a pre-industrial society, based largely on mutual support and paternal protection of the lower orders, was gradually eroded and replaced by a more individualistic and less caring society.

As the ties of the eighteenth century weakened, and the industrial revolution gained momentum, one key issue emerged. If the self-made man was regarded as the most competent and virtuous member of society, why should he be excluded from the franchise? Up until 1832, both the middle and lower classes shared a common objective: to introduce a more representative system of government. Inspired by revolutions in America and France, as well as by the ideas of men such as Paine and Mill, their arguments acquired a legitimacy which was hard to refute.

2 The Liberty Tree: the American and French Revolutions

The American and French Revolutions provided a spur to discussion and debate about the nature of liberty and political independence. While the Whig oligarchy of the eighteenth century appeared relatively stable, even before the bid for independence by Britain's American colonies, liberal ideas concerning representation and the reform of the constitution had been circulating. The American Revolution stimu-lated a more powerful critique of the monarchy and the role of the aristocracy. Consequently, reformers questioned more closely the precise principles of the Revolution Settlement of 1688: was it sufficient that the monarch and Parliament should govern on behalf of the many when so few had the right to select their representatives?

The Dissenters were notable critics of the existing constitution. They consisted of various religious groups, such as the Methodists and Presbyterians, which refused to conform to the laws of the Anglican Church. Their leader, Richard Price, argued in 1789 that, according to the Revolution Settlement, the King only ruled by consent. If the monarch abused his powers then the people were entitled to with-draw their support. According to Price, there was a social contract between governor and governed, whereby the latter had the inalien-able right to choose the former. In America, however, that contract had broken down. The British Government had tried to enforce taxa-tion of the colonies without granting them rights of parliamentary representation. This was condemned as an infringement of liberty, with George III perceived as the source of that tyranny and abso-lutism. The Revolution of 1688 had conserved the monarchy but now it had abused its powers, reneged on its contract with its subjects, and had to be reformed or replaced.

American independence proved that political reform was attain-able - a Republican government upheld the principles of democracy, guaranteed in the form of a written constitution. British reformers

could contrast a government based on consent and their own hereditary monarchy which restricted political rights to a minority. Other
features of the new republic were also attractive. America had
addressed the evils of patronage by removing the property qualification as a prerequisite for public office. The whole status of the individual changed from that of a *subject* of the Crown to that of a *citizen*.
The first implied that one was beholden to one's superiors and ultimately the monarch; the latter suggested a position of equality within
society. Finally, the democratic ideal was secured by the introduction
of universal suffrage. The American Revolution, therefore, gave fresh
impetus to the debate among British reformers, with issues such as
republicanism, a more popular constitution, as well as a wider franchise central to their campaign.

Further inspiration occurred in 1789, with the onset of the French
Revolution. The platform of demands articulated during the 1770s
and 1780s gained a sense of greater urgency, with the rhetoric of some
reformers becoming more extreme. Increasingly the discussion
concentrated on the need for government by consent, on civil liberty
and adult male suffrage. Dissenters contributed to the campaign,
acutely critical of their exclusion from public office because of the
restrictions imposed by the Test and Corporation Acts. These stipu-
lated that an oath had to be sworn acknowledging the supremacy of
the monarch as head of Church and State. Holy Communion
according the the rites of the Church of England had to be taken
before an individual could assume public office. Inevitably this
debarred all Catholics, non-Anglicans and Jews. Although the
Protestant succession had been secured by the Revolution Settlement,
fears of anti-Protestant movements governed contemporary attitudes.
But the pressure to relax these restraints was intrinsically linked with
the campaign for political reform, Dissenters frequently being the
driving force behind efforts to reform Parliament and thereby gain
civil and religious liberties. Thus many Dissenters had joined the
Revolution Society on the grounds that it sought to highlight the principles of government enshrined in the Revolution Settlement of 1688.
The fact that these principles had yet to be enacted was the thesis of a
famous address by Richard Price to the Society for Commemorating
the Revolution in Great Britain on 4 November 1789:

1   But the most important instance of the imperfect state in which the
     Revolution left our constitution, is the INEQUALITY OF OUR REPRE-
     SENTATION. I think, indeed, this defect in our constitution so gross and
     so palpable, as to make it excellent chiefly in form and theory … When
5   the representation is fair and equal, and at the same time vested with
     such powers as our House of Commons possesses, a kingdom may be
     said to govern itself, and consequently to possess true liberty. When the
     representation is partial, a kingdom possesses liberty only partially; and
     if extremely partial, it only gives a *semblance* of liberty; but if not only

10 extremely partial, but corruptly chosen, and under corrupt influence
after being chosen, it becomes a *nuisance* and produces the worst of all
forms of government - a government by corruption....
    The inadequacies of our representation has been long a subject of
complaint. This is, in truth, our fundamental grievance; and I do not think
15 that any thing is much more our duty, as men who love their country,
and who are grateful for the Revolution, than to unite our zeal in
endeavouring to get it redressed.[2]

Price's speech was a radical exposition of all that was perceived to be
at fault in the British constitution. His outspoken condemnation of
corruption and inadequate representation signified a total disrespect
for the current government. In his opinion, liberty could only be
guaranteed if representation in Parliament was 'fair and equal'.
    Clearly the French Revolution was a critical factor in inspiring polit-
ical reaction in Britain. But the idealistic fervour which accompanied
the early stages soon dissipated once news of the Terror, in which
thousands of innocent French people were executed for their alleged
opposition to the Revolution, reached England. Critics of the
Revolution felt vindicated, their dire warnings on the perils of democracy now justified. They could afford to be complacent, sure that the
existing British constitution merited preservation. However, as seen
in the political cartoon published in 1798 (see opposite), their opponents were scornful that members of the establishment were content
to see all the faults of 'Old England' continue unchallenged. The
French Revolution, and its American precursor, had ignited a debate
which continued for several decades.

3 Political Writers

The third factor which influenced political reform in Britain was the
impact of various political writers. Their intellectual ideas generated
wide-ranging discussion which in turn raised expectations about the
future nature of democratic government.

a) The Revolutionary Era

i) Thomas Paine
One of the more outspoken radical campaigners was Thomas Paine,
whose views helped to shape the reform debate. Paine had become
increasingly dissatisfied with political life in England and was particularly critical of the powers exerted by the British monarchy. In
1774, he sailed to Philadelphia, where the American colonists were
already seeking to establish their rights to liberty. Paine quickly
appreciated that here was a sympathetic environment in which he
could publicise his growing dislike of the British monarchy. During
the period of the American Revolution, Paine wrote a number of

May the British Constitution *never be repaired with the* Plaister of Paris

Woodward Delin

Published Oct 29 1798 by R Ackerman 101 Strand

A Toast for Old England.

A political cartoon, 29 October 1798

significant pamphlets and essays on the subject of democracy. For example, in his pamphlet *Common Sense*, published in January 1776, he openly attacked the principle of hereditary monarchy and argued the merits of a republic as an alternative. In 1783, he praised the way revolution had 'contributed more to enlighten the world, and diffuse a spirit of freedom and liberality among mankind than any human event ... that ever preceded it'.[3] By the time Paine left the United States in 1787 and sailed to France, America had, in his opinion, successfully acquired all the attributes of sound government (see pages 16-17).

Once in France, Paine witnessed the drama of the French Revolution. Just as he had supported the Americans in rejecting British rule, so now he urged the French to adopt republicanism and an equal franchise. The revolutionary events in France provided vital impetus to the forum of debate in Britain. Paine seized this opportunity to reiterate his thoughts on republicanism, ever hopeful that Britain would follow the path of America and France and defeat the tyranny of the British monarchy.

One of his most famous contributions to the revolutionary debate was his book *The Rights of Man*, first published in 1791. The second part, published in February 1792, launched strong attacks on the principle of a hereditary monarchy. His argument focused on the premise that Britain was ruled by a corrupt government, headed by a monarchy which had conquered Britain in 1066. Norman despotism was guilty of destroying ancient English liberties:

1 ... a race of conquerors arose, whose Government, like that of William the Conqueror, was founded in power, and the sword assumed the name of a sceptre. Governments thus established last as long as the power to support them lasts; but that they might avail themselves of
5 every engine in their favour, they united fraud to force, and set up an idol which they called *Divine Right*, and which, in imitation of the Pope, who affects to be spiritual and temporal, and in contradiction to the Founder of the Christian religion, twisted itself afterwards into an idol of another shape, called *Church and State*. The key of St Peter and the
10 key of the Treasury became quartered on one another, and the wondering cheated multitude worshipped the invention.[4]

Paine had no respect for a monarchy whose authority had been established by force and which had then created the concept of Divine Right, whereby the monarch was the spiritual representative of God on earth. In establishing his supremacy both as political and spiritual leader, the monarch was bestowing upon himself a degree of absolute power which could not be challenged. This absolutism was the source of corruption because it could not be restrained.

The other key component of Paine's argument was the concept of natural rights and civil rights. Paine believed that an individual had natural rights which he or she automatically acquired at birth and which no government could violate. He had the authority to exercise those basic rights such as to eat, clothe and protect himself. However, once the individual became part of a society, he had to recognise that other rules were also necessary in order to ensure a harmonious existence. These rules might necessitate forsaking some natural rights because they conflicted with the common good. Nevertheless, Paine believed that individuals would willingly respect a set of rules if they were the result of consultation and consent between rulers and ruled. By becoming a member of such a society, the individual would acquire civil rights, which included the right to be consulted about the nature of government.

Paine's ideology thus embraced a radically new concept which rejected all notion of political rights being dependent on the ownership of property. Equal political rights were an intrinsic entitlement for all men. His political vision of manhood suffrage challenged the status quo of late eighteenth-century Britain at a time when the government was highly nervous of revolution. The considerable popularity of his *The Rights of Man* seemed conclusive proof to the authorities that Britain was in danger of political upheaval. Yet whilst Paine championed the cause of liberty and citizens' rights, he also prompted a divergence within the radical movement. His writings represented the extreme wing of radical thought and for many other reformers his notoriety was too controversial.

ii) Edmund Burke

Paine was not the only political thinker to appreciate the implications of revolution in France. Into the melting pot of rhetorical arguments poured a wide range of ideas, all serving to create a lively debate on issues of reform. Like many reformers, Edmund Burke had regarded the Revolution of 1688 as having established the key principles of constitutional government. Yet his interpretation of those principles did not necessarily accord with the views of his contemporaries. He was, for example, very critical of the Revolution Society and of Richard Price's speech on 4 November 1789, claiming that Price had misinterpreted the meaning of the 1688 Revolution. Price argued that Parliament, by choosing a new monarch to replace James II, had negated the principle of hereditary monarchy.

Burke was appalled by this claim. The appointment of William III had been a necessity, an exception to the rule, in order to secure the Protestant succession. In his book *Reflections on the French Revolution and Other Essays* (1790), Burke scorned Price's ideas.

1   His doctrines affect our constitution in its vital parts. He tells the Revolution Society in this political sermon, that his Majesty 'is almost the *only* lawful king in the world, because the *only* one who owes his crown to the *choice of his people*' ...

5   This doctrine, as applied to the prince now on the British throne,

either is nonsense, and therefore neither true nor false, or it affirms a most unfounded, dangerous, illegal and unconstitutional position. According to this spiritual doctor of politics, if his Majesty does not owe his crown to the choice of his people, he is no *lawful king*.[5]

In Burke's view, 1688 was not a democratic revolution but one which re-established stability. It was now essential to preserve the merits of Britain's constitution in order to protect Britain from the dangers of democracy.

It was the dramatic events in France which prompted Burke to write his book and which provoked such a divergence of views. Paine had been inspired by the French *Declaration of the Rights of Man*, which enshrined the principles of individual liberty and citizenship. In contrast, Burke believed that the liberty of men still had to be restrained because they were bound by a contract between governors and governed. Unlike Paine, Burke did not adhere to the concept that the people had an automatic right to renounce the conditions of the contract. Thus when France issued the *Declaration of the Rights of Man*, Burke denounced it as 'anarchy',[6] believing that it would provoke all the dangerous elements of democracy. It was essential to restrain the '*swinish multitude*'.[7]

Another fundamental idea of Burke's was the belief that the existing composition of the English constitution produced secure government. Its ideal combination of monarchy, aristocracy and the House of Commons guaranteed ancient privileges, liberties and franchises. Alarmed by the democratic nature of the Revolution in France, Burke praised England's institutions as evidence of stable and wise government.

Burke had hoped that a liberal-minded aristocracy in France would successfully shape the outcome of the Revolution, establishing values akin to those of the Whig monarchy in Britain. These hopes were soon dashed. Burke rapidly came to distrust the lawless nature of the French Revolution and reasserted his support for conservative principles, on the grounds that it was too dangerous to grant men equal political rights. Burke's reflections on the French Revolution, whilst not necessarily typical of his radical contemporaries, were significant for several reasons. They paved the way for a more measured response to the French Revolution. They also provided a legitimate basis for government opposition to Paine's book and consequently a determination to resist democracy.

b) The Post-Revolutionary Era

Like Burke, many Whig reformers had reacted with some confusion to the French Revolution, their support for a democratic movement tempered by their dislike of violence. Although many were not prepared to endorse the views of Paine, there remained a strong groundswell of opinion which hoped that parliamentary reform in Britain would gain some impetus. Thus the issues of hereditary monarchy, the constitution and the rights of individuals remained the focal point of radical thought and writings. More significantly, as the furore over the threat of revolution from France receded, the theoretical principles of these ideas could be discussed more rationally and with a greater degree of consensus. It is clear that these ideas were a contributory factor in helping to shape the unique form of democracy in Britain.

i) James Mill

Two prominent writers in the post-revolutionary period were James Mill and Jeremy Bentham. Mill's thoughts provided a vital new dimension to the debate about democracy. Unsettled by the radicalism of Paine, the reform movement had to re-establish credibility and unity. This was not easy, especially during the period after 1815 when there was considerable support for the radical ideas propounded by Henry Hunt, based on the principle of universal suffrage (see page 2). Yet with the collapse of popular radicalism in 1820, a more careful articulation of democratic ideals was required which could appeal to a wider audience.

Mill's writings in many ways echoed the thoughts of both Price and Paine. There was, for example, the now familiar attack on the extent to which government had undermined the principles of the Revolution Settlement of 1688. In an article for the *Edinburgh Review* in 1809, Mill argued that 1688 had guaranteed people's liberties and given them the right to resist oppression. Yet these rights were now threatened by a subsequent increase in the power of the aristocracy, who were taking advantage of their predominance in Parliament to implement unfair taxation and repressive laws. These intrinsic rights were being infringed by such laws as the Seditious Meetings Act passed in 1795, which limited public gatherings at the discretion of local magistrates.

Mill offered a harsh criticism of aristocratic government in his *Essays on Government* (1825). He likened the existing structure of government to a number of clubs whose membership consisted of landlords, merchants, manufacturers, officers from the army and navy, and lawyers who had

I   unlimited power over the whole community put into their hands. These clubs have, each, and all of them, an interest, an interest the same with that which governs all other rulers, in mismanagement, in converting the persons and properties of the rest of the community wholly to their 5   own benefit ...

If the powers of Government are placed in the hands of persons whose interests are not identified with those of the community, the interests of the community are wholly sacrificed to those of the rulers ...[8]

It was this 'motley aristocracy' that Mill denigrated so forcefully. As with Paine, he could see no merit in such an unrepresentative form of government; but he digressed from Paine's views in one significant way. He claimed that it was the middle ranks who were the most 'intelligent', 'wise' and 'virtuous' members of society. It was they who would act wisely in 'the management of public affairs' and it was to them that the lower ranks would defer for 'advice and assistance'. It would be from these ranks that good government would emanate. Essentially, Mill was an advocate of granting the suffrage to the middle classes because they would act in the interests of those beneath them.

In departing from the principle of universal suffrage, Mill provided the Radical movement with a more moderate political philosophy, but one which might appeal to a wider audience. His arguments proved particularly attractive during the Reform crisis of 1832. The crux of Mill's ideas was that government had two alternatives: to face anarchy or to govern by consent. The first would occur if the government resisted reform. In such circumstances the press could exacerbate the threat of revolution so as to make it seem an imminent danger. Alternatively, the government could opt for peaceful constitutional change, persuaded, as Mill believed, by the weight of public opinion expressed through a free press. It was this philosophy which underlay much of the campaign waged by the middle classes during the reform crisis of 1830-2 (see pages 38-41). Although the Whigs' decision to extend the franchise in 1832 was clearly influenced by political expediency, it was significant that the people enfranchised were the very group who Mill argued could be trusted to be loyal to the country's institutions.

ii) Jeremy Bentham

Another key figure in the transition from the era of pre-French revolutionary radicalism to that of early Victorian Britain was Jeremy Bentham, whose political philosophy became a cornerstone of radical thought in Britain during the 1820s and 1830s. As with Mill, there are elements of continuity in his ideas with those of previous political writers. Like his fellow radical thinkers, Bentham had reacted positively to the earlier stages of the French Revolution, optimistic that parliamentary reform in Britain would ensue. However, it was the excesses of the events in France which prompted Bentham to modify his views. Hence in the post-revolutionary period a very distinctive radicalism emerged, one which was tempered by a concern to avoid the anarchic tendencies of democracy. With Bentham, the more moderate ideas of political philosophy were consolidated and it was these thoughts which became more typical of Victorian political ideology.

Bentham had become convinced that Britain's government was despotic due to the monopoly exercised by the monarchy and the aristocracy. The Crown exercised patronage in the interests of the political elite whilst the legal system was controlled by the landed interest, whose members ensured that they and Members of Parliament were the chief beneficiaries of legislation. These abuses could be eliminated if more direct control of the monarch by the people was implemented. The monarch's function was 'only to appoint from time to time such ministers as were indicated to him ... by the voice of the people faithfully represented in parliament'.[9]

Fundamental to this belief was the premise that government was a trust between the government and the people. Yet how could that trust be preserved in a way which guaranteed people's rights and liberties without endangering sound government? In Bentham's view, the *Declaration of the Rights of Man* had introduced a dangerous concept of democracy. It gave power to people without property, thereby undermining the general interest of the whole community. Wise government must protect property, as this ensured economic prosperity. Too much equality would threaten even the interests of the poorer classes. Their livelihood was more secure, Bentham argued, under a system which upheld property. Bentham's interpretation of democracy was nonetheless radical as it challenged many of the existing assumptions about the right to vote. He proposed

1   to institute universal suffrage, ... 'to admit to a participation in the election suffrage, all such persons as, being of the male sex, of mature age, and of sound mind, shall, during a determinate time antecedent to the day of the election, have been resident either as householders or
5   inmates, within the district or place in which they are called to vote';-the secret ballot;- a fresh election at least once a year ...[10]

In addition, he suggested equal electoral districts and elections held on only one day in order to prevent corruption. These ideas were advanced for their time, although Bentham's notion of universal suffrage essentially meant household suffrage. These ideas were soon reiterated as part of the People's Charter (see page 42), but were not incorporated as basic democratic principles until later in the century.

One of Bentham's most important contributions to political thought was his theory of utilitarianism. Utilitarianism was the doctrine that society should be organised so as to ensure 'the greatest happiness of the greatest number'. This entailed creating a suitable balance between permitting individuals to pursue their own best interests, and hence their personal happiness, and guaranteeing the happiness of the wider community. The government had a dual role in protecting the rights of the individual on the one hand, but also judging whether individual actions in pursuit of happiness might infringe the interests of society as a whole. Yet there was a danger that governments would abuse their rights to judge the needs of society unless they, the governors, were directly accountable to the people they served. Bentham argued that universal suffrage was the best protector against abuse of power. By applying the principle of utilitarianism, the people would be able to ensure that the public interest, the interest of the greatest number, was best preserved. An appropriate balance between sound government and the rights of the people would be achieved.

Bentham's philosophy appealed greatly to the increasingly prosperous middle classes. He sought to attain a balance between collective responsibility and individual autonomy. Not only did he advocate the protection of property, a principle dear to those beneficiaries of capitalism, but he also endeavoured to increase government responsibility, a principle subsequently reflected in legislation, such as the Poor Law Amendment Act, as well as public health policy. Such legislation seemed to secure the very objectives of the middle classes - the pursuit of the interests of the majority, efficient administration, but with some scope for individualism.

c) The Mid-Victorian Era

i) John Stuart Mill and Walter Bagehot

Bentham's contributions to political and social theory are widely seen as precursors of Victorian liberalism. By 1867, his views had not only been incorporated into much of government policy, they had also influenced subsequent political theory, especially the ideas of two key mid-Victorian philosophers, J.S. Mill, son of James Mill, and Walter Bagehot. By the middle years of the century, political thought had lost the radical, almost revolutionary tone of the earlier years. The middle classes no longer needed to justify their claim to political power. That had been accorded to them in 1832, and as the prosperous years of mid-Victorian England enhanced their value as members of society, so they could afford to consider possible political rewards for those whose hard labour had contributed to that prosperity. The key question which dominated political discussion from 1864 onwards was how to extend the franchise further whilst still protecting property.

Both J.S. Mill and Walter Bagehot saw the need for checks and balances within the constitution. Mill argued in *Considerations on Representative Government* (1865) that only those deemed worthy of the responsibility should be enfranchised. Mill asserted that

1   ... the assembly which votes the taxes ... should be elected exclusively by those who pay something towards the taxes imposed.... That representation should be coextensive with taxation, not stopping short of it, but also going beyond it, is in accordance with the theory of British insti-
5   tutions.[11]

Whilst proclaiming the need for a more liberal constitution, Mill still feared the dangers of mediocrity, with the government being weakened by a levelling down of standards. Thus it can be seen that the morality of mid-Victorian Britain pervaded political thought. Neither men such as Mill nor their political representatives could contemplate a democracy which did not preserve the influence of the educated and protect against ignorance. Those individuals who were not respected, such as those on poor relief, could not be entrusted with the vote. By 1867, therefore, the arguments of the post-French revolutionary thinkers had clearly prevailed. Paine's notion of natural rights had been rejected in favour of the values and expectations of the middle classes.

Bagehot, writing in 1867, likewise cautioned against the dangers of full democracy. The masses were too ignorant to exercise political power wisely. Instead, Bagehot came to epitomise another familiar value of Victorian England, that of deference to one's superiors. Exclusion of the masses could be justified on the grounds that the lower classes were naturally respectful of, or deferential to, those above them and therefore accepted without question the right of the middle and upper classes to rule. Just as Mill expected voters to be able to read, write and pay taxes, so Bagehot felt it essential to restrict the franchise to those who were educated. Both Mill and Bagehot exemplified the reason why Britain was able to sustain the dominance of the middle classes when other European countries experienced upheaval and revolution. Their political philosophies provided a suitable framework within which politicians could comfortably consider political reform without risking the experiences of their European neighbours.

4 Conclusion: Britain in 1868

Between 1780 and 1868 there were a number of long-term influences, external and internal, which challenged, undermined, and finally altered the power structure in Britain. A limited, oligarchic government was ultimately replaced by a government which embraced the ideas and principles of the middle class. Although the institutions of government (monarchy, House of Lords and House of Commons) remained unchanged, the balance of power within had shifted noticeably. The old ties of allegiance which had epitomised the hierarchical power structure in Britain had been weakened. By 1868 it had become acceptable to admit the urban working class within the constitution, a concept unthinkable in 1780. In addition, that change had occurred without any violent struggle.

How had it been possible for the narrow and very selective form of representation which had been the hallmark of eighteenth-century politics to have been replaced by a much wider and more democratic system? A major factor was clearly the impact of the Industrial Revolution. As Britain took on the mantle of a leading manufacturing country, so Britain's ruling landed elite was compelled to recognise the economic significance of the middle classes. The government's response was reflected in the economic policies of the 1820s onwards, when taxes on imports were relaxed and free trade was encouraged. Individualism, the entrepreneurial spirit, coupled with minimum government intervention, flourished in the new competitive world. It was recognised that the authors of Britain's growing wealth deserved a more significant reward. As a result, they had to address the crucial question of how to define the political role of the middle classes. As will be seen in Chapter 3, the expansion of the franchise was never intended as some great democratic act. So whilst the Industrial Revolution persuaded the aristocracy that they had to accommodate the middle classes, a system of government had to be devised which did not endanger Britain's institutions and which maintained the aristocracy's hold on the reins of power.

What is so distinctive about the democracy which developed in Britain during the first half of the nineteenth century is that it was achieved without the confrontational power struggles experienced in America and France. The American and French Revolutions were instrumental in intensifying the level of political debate in Britain. Both illustrated the viability of questioning supposedly archaic systems of government; both provided practical evidence of constitutional reform. However, for most British members of government and political reformers alike, the violence associated with these revolutions was something to be condemned and avoided. Many gladly welcomed the principles of reform but not the method.

The fact that Britain's institutions of government remained intact is an indication of the degree of political expediency exercised by the governing classes, which influenced the process of reform. Revolution was averted because the values of the middle classes, the strong work ethic and *laissez-faire* economics, were included in government legislation. Civil liberties were granted. Likewise, the political worth of the middle classes was recognised because political thinkers had managed to influence the direction of reform. Writers such as Paine, Burke, James Mill, Bentham, J.S. Mill and Bagehot articulated the concerns and aspirations of those people who sought to remedy a deficient system of representation. Their writings provided a framework within which ideas regarding the future political role of the middle classes could evolve. Their ideas were sufficiently flexible to accommodate the continuously changing nature of British society.

In conclusion, a number of key features of nineteenth-century Britain are now identifiable - peaceful constitutional reform, civil liberties, minimum government interference, *laissez-faire* economics, free trade and individualism. All were essential ingredients of a political creed which dominated nineteenth-century Britain, namely liberalism. These ideas had clearly evolved over a long period of time. However, the effects of the Industrial Revolution, the American and French Revolutions, the actions of those in power and the writings of political thinkers all contributed towards consolidating liberalism as the main political philosophy of nineteenth-century Britain. It was liberalism which shaped and sustained Britain's distinctive form of parliamentary government. Liberalism survived because its central beliefs were so attractive to the chief beneficiaries of political and economic reform, the middle classes. Liberalism was only threatened once the full effects of greater political involvement were felt at the end of the nineteenth century. Only then did people begin to question whether liberalism really served the interests of *all* individuals.

References
1 Harold Perkin, *Origins of Modern English Society* (Routledge, 1969), p.62.
2 Cited in M. Butler, *Burke, Paine, Godwin and the Revolutionary Controversy* (Cambridge University Press, 1984), pp.30-1.
3 Crisis No. 13, April 1783, cited in David Freeman Hawke, *Paine* (William Norton, 1992), p.135.
4 Thomas Paine, *The Rights of Man*, edited by Tony Benn (Everyman, 1993), p.35.
5 Edmund Burke, *Reflections on the French Revolution and Other Essays* (J.M. Dent & Son, 1940), pp.11-12.
6 Hawke, *Paine*, p.202.
7 Ibid, p.218.
8 James Mill, *Essays on Government, Jurisprudence, Liberty of the Press and Law of Nations* (Routledge, 1992), pp.25, 28.
9 Cited in J.R. Dinwiddy, 'Bentham's Transition to Political Radicalism, 1809-10', *Journal of the History of Ideas*, 1975, vol.36, 1975, p.693.
10 Cited in Elie Halevy, *The Growth of Philosophic Radicalism* (Faber and Faber, 1952), p.263.
11 J.S. Mill, 'Considerations on Representative Government' in John Gray (ed), *John Stuart Mill, On Liberty and Other Essays* (Oxford University Press, 1998), pp.331-2.

Answering essay questions on 'External and Internal Challenges 1780-1867'

Exam questions on political reform often require either a broad analysis of long-term factors, or will focus on more immediate historical influences. For the former, the following questions might arise:

1. How and why did perceptions of 'democracy' in Britain change between 1780 and 1867?
2. How far were contemporary political thinkers influential in shaping British democracy between 1780 and 1867?
3. To what extent did the Industrial Revolution affect political development in Britain during the first half of the nineteenth century?
4. Why did 'aristocratic' government give way to government by the middle classes?
5. Evaluate the contribution of the following to the emergence of democracy in Britain between 1780 and 1867:
    (i) The American and French Revolutions

(ii) The Industrial Revolution
(iii) Political thinkers.

There are several golden rules to follow when writing a history essay. Firstly, read the question carefully, and make sure you understand its meaning. Many mistakes are made at this stage by students who misinterpret the question and write irrelevant answers on a different question. Secondly, spend a few minutes writing an essay plan. Here you should outline all the key points which you think are pertinent to the question. Make sure that (i) they are in a logical order, (ii) you have appropriate evidence to support each point and (iii) they form coherent links in an overall argument. A good essay plan will enable you to write an apropriate introduction, a well-argued and relevant main section, followed by a balanced conclusion. Each of these stages will be discussed in this book.

Your introduction is a vital section of your essay and your first task is to analyse and define the question set. Some questions will ask you to assess a historical issue, with phrases like 'how far', 'to what extent', or 'how effective was'. Both questions 2 and 3 are assessment questions. Or, the question could ask for an explanation, e.g. 'why', 'account for', 'how and why'. Questions 1 and 4 both require explanations.

Next you should ensure that you understand the main focus of the question so that you can include a brief explanation of what the question is about in your introduction. With Question 2, for example, you would need to define the main terms of the question, 'contemporary political thinkers'. Suggest who you think should be included - Paine, Bentham, James Mill, J.S. Mill? Make sure that your evaluation will be comprehensive. Next, recognise that you have to assess or evaluate their role in shaping British democracy between 1780 and 1867. Your introduction should indicate an awareness that their influence can only be assessed in comparison with the role of other factors. Some brief reference to these factors - economic, political and social - will be needed. Above all, keep the introduction succinct and precise.

Summary Diagram
External and Internal Challenges, 1780-1868

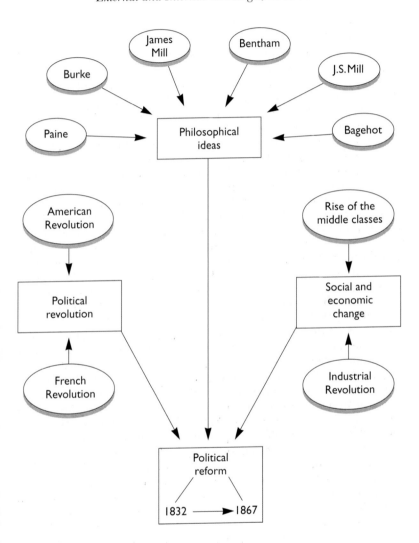

3 Government and the People, 1780-1868

Famous Whig historians of the nineteenth century such as Thomas Macaulay argued that Britain's history was a unique story of progress towards liberal democracy. The country's constitution was strengthened by the successful survival of its parliamentary institutions. Such significant political events as the 1688 Settlement and the 1832 Reform Act were stabilising factors, facilitating change without the need for bloodshed. Macaulay emphasised the greatness of Britain's constitutional past claiming that it was the far-sighted actions of Britain's ruling class which managed to preserve the very best features of parliamentary government.

This thesis, largely endorsed by historians such as W. Molesworth and G.M. Trevelyan, is part of the traditional Whig view of history. But historians have questioned its simplistic analysis. History is not shaped merely by the actions of the ruling classes. The Marxist historian E.P. Thompson, for example, asserted that we should examine more closely the contribution of the working classes in providing pressure for change. Thompson's research was an inspiration for subsequent historians to study the history of Britain's 'under-classes'. As a result, there is now a wealth of research which offers a wide range of explanations for the development of democracy in Britain between 1780 and 1868.

Chapter 2 described a number of fundamental long-term influences on the growth of liberal democracy in Britain - the social and economic effects of the Industrial Revolution, the political revolutions in America and France and changing political philosophies. As a result, the concept of liberalism underpinned parliamentary government in nineteenth-century Britain. But to what extent was Britain democratic by 1868 and were there other, more immediate factors which were crucial to Britain's political development? The first major reform, as indicated in Chapter 2, was the 1832 Reform Act, in which the Whigs admitted the middle classes to the suffrage. The second, the 1867 Reform Act, passed by the Conservatives, enfranchised the urban working class. Although each reform was only a small step towards greater democracy, collectively they were a major achievement. So were the Whigs and Tories, as architects of these reforms, motivated by principles or pragmatism? How significant were their changes in attitude in facilitating political change? Reform was an interactive process. Pressure from the grass-roots often alarmed the government, but was, nevertheless, a key element in determining the emergence of democracy. This chapter will analyse all three factors, the reforms, the political parties and the role of the people, in order to reach an understanding about how and why liberal democracy developed in Britain.

The campaign for democratic reform can be analysed in three

stages: 1780-1820, 1821-48 and 1849-68. The first was characterised by the dominance of conservative attitudes, provoked by fears of revolution, in conflict with radical political activity. The second saw a gradual modification of intransigent positions as the Whigs, in particular, granted concessions to the middle classes. Despite continual protest from the working class, namely the Chartists (see pages 41-43), by the end of 1848 a more stable equilibrium between different political and social groups was emerging. Finally, between 1849 and 1868, as the beneficial effects of the Industrial Revolution materialised, that stability was consolidated. As a result, the prospect of enfranchising the working class became a reality.

1 1780-1820: Conservatism versus Radicalism

a) The Key 'Players'

The American and French Revolutions had a major impact on Britain's main political parties, the Tories and the Whigs, as well as the radicals seeking reform. All three groups were key 'players' in either encouraging or resisting demands for political change in Britain. How did each group react?

The response of the Tories to the revolutionary events in America and France was influenced by long-held beliefs and attitudes. The Tories were notable for their patriotism, support for law and order, and their intrinsic belief in the traditional institutions of the country: the Crown, the Church, and Parliament. As members of the aristocratic class, the majority of Tories approved of a hierarchical society in which they were the natural leaders. Maintenance of rank was an essential prerequisite to political stability. These attitudes were blatantly exposed during the period of the American and French Revolutions. The Tories were determined to protect England from the dangers of democracy, and therefore shared the conservative ideals of Edmund Burke (see page 21-22). Their reaction to subsequent events reflected these deeply held convictions.

The Whigs were divided in their response to the revolutions. Like the Tories, they were a largely aristocratic party, and so shared the Tories' concern to protect property. But they were also a more cosmopolitan party, attracting political reformers, nonconformists (religious dissenters) and middle-class manufacturers. These Whigs were more critical of the country's established institutions because they appeared to obstruct progress. In particular, they believed that the Crown had abused its authority. Both the American and French Revolutions, therefore, gave encouragement to those Whigs who sought to restrain the Crown and to reform the constitution. More conservative Whigs reacted with alarm to events abroad, convinced that the excesses displayed in France revealed all the inherent dangers of democracy. The threat to the landed classes had to be averted.

The most positive response to the American and French Revolutions came from the radical reformers who, inspired by the progress of democracy in these countries and by the literature of writers such as Tom Paine (see pages 18-21), believed that reform could be implemented in Britain. Yet at the end of the eighteenth century, most of the protest was led by middle-class organisations such as the Society for Constitutional Information and the Westminster Association, whose six demands consisted of universal manhood suffrage, equal-sized constituencies, annual parliaments, the secret ballot, the payment of MPs and the abolition of the property qualification for MPs. Their aims were not to destroy private property but to remove what they perceived as despotic government, founded on privilege and oligarchical control, to reform unfair taxation and to establish a more representative parliament.

The Corresponding Societies were also widely supported. The first society, the London Corresponding Society founded in London in January 1792, attracted literate, skilled artisans such as Thomas Hardy, a shoemaker, and Francis Place, a tailor. Provincial societies, such as one in Sheffield, soon proliferated. As with the Society for Constitutional Information, the methodology of protest was a familiar pattern of printing and selling broadsheets, pamphlets, conducting debates and holding political meetings with the hope of eliciting support for reform. Yet the Corresponding Societies were not a revolutionary movement. As artisans, they too were often small property owners and so saw little purpose in either endorsing the more radical aims of Thomas Paine or copying the actions of the French Jacobins.

b) Confrontation

As the effects of the French Revolution reverberated across the English Channel, so all the key 'players' became embroiled in a process of confrontation which did not abate until 1820. Yet the fact that radical protesters did not resort to violent protest on any large scale is fundamental to understanding why Britain evolved such a distinctive form of parliamentary democracy. The language of radicals was often revolutionary in tone, but their actions fell short of destabilising the government. Nevertheless, there were periods when the government was confronted with serious problems of disorder. However, the government's successful containment of those threats, combined with the absence of large-scale genuine revolutionary intentions, helped to avert any repetition of events in France.

The first period of confrontation, during the 1780s and 1790s, was one of extreme reactions by both politicians and the people. Radicals pursued their goals of parliamentary reform by holding meetings nationwide in the hope of spreading political awareness amongst their supporters. Public agitation peaked in 1795 with two large demonstrations, both held despite increasing harassment from the authorities. Alarmed by the popularity of Paine's book, and the growth of radical activity, the Tory government had adopted a policy of suppression. *Habeas Corpus*, which gives any individual the right to be formally charged with a crime if arrested, was twice suspended during the 1790s, so permitting the imprisonment of radicals without trial. Government spies infiltrated radical organisations, often exaggerating radical activity in order to justify the arrest of prominent leaders. Charges of seditious libel, whereby individuals were accused of inciting unlawful insurrection, followed by trial and imprisonment, were a frequent means of curtailing radical activity. The government was convinced that they faced the threat of a revolutionary conspiracy and consequently they over-reacted.

By the start of the nineteenth century, government action had successfully suppressed most radical protest. It was not until shortly before the conclusion of the Napoleonic Wars in 1815 that Britain saw a revival of radical protest whose origins were closely linked with the other key long-term influence on political change, the Industrial Revolution. Framework knitters were particularly hit by the relaxation of paternalistic legislation protecting trades and by the imposition of *laissez-faire* economics (see page 15). Furthermore, their skills were undermined by new machines, their wages undercut by unskilled labour. Hit by a severe depression between 1811 and 1813, they sought redress for their grievances from Parliament. Once their complaints were rejected, they resorted to more radical methods of expressing their discontent, namely the breaking of machines. Supposedly led by a man called Ned Lud, the Luddites posed a fresh challenge to the Tory Government. The Tories' response was predictable. Troops were deployed to break up the strikes, and a total of 16 Luddites were executed for their involvement in the protests.

The Tories felt unable to relax their policies lest they released the dangerous forces of democracy which so far they had successfully contained. The combination, therefore, of severe economic conditions and repressive government created a potentially inflammatory situation. This was compounded by the fact that, between 1815 and 1820, the post-war radical movement became more politicised. Inspired by its charismatic leader, Henry Hunt, the movement advocated universal manhood suffrage. Hunt's willingness to use methods of mass pressure rather than petition and debate signified a more confrontational approach to obtaining a programme of democratic reform. The rhetoric of the reformers had a familiar theme: democratic control was the essential prerequisite to economic improvement; good government would be restored as soon as people's rights were upheld under the constitution. These objectives motivated the supporters of Hunt, but the outcome of their protests often resulted in conflict between them and the authorities.

Of all the various protests, the Peterloo Massacre, August 1819, was the most renowned. In the month preceding the Peterloo Massacre, one of the outspoken journals, *The Black Dwarf*, owned by T. Wooler, reported the proceedings at the Leeds Reform meeting at which reformers demanded democratic reform.

1   That as we are perfectly satisfied that Annual Parliaments and Universal Suffrage, constitute essential parts of our Constitution, and are our rightful inheritance; we shall consider our grievances unredressed, and our indisputable rights withheld from us, until we are possessed of such
5   Annual Parliaments and Universal Suffrage ...
    That, whenever oppression or despotism militates against, or is the ruin of the one, it must in the end be the destruction of the other; we therefore entreat them ... ere it should be too late, to stand forward and espouse the constitutional rights of the people, by obtaining a
10 Radical Reform in the system of Representation, which alone can save both the trading and labouring classes from ruin.[1]

When unarmed men, women and children gathered at St. Peter's Field near Manchester to support the demand for parliamentary reform, local magistrates ordered the yeomanry to disperse the crowds. Despite over 400 injured and 11 dead, the government congratulated the magistrates' decision and refused to hold a public inquiry. Subsequent legislation reiterated the government's intent to suppress popular protest.

In November 1819, the Foreign Secretary, Lord Castlereagh, introduced the Seditious Meetings Prevention Bill in the House of Commons, claiming that

1   ... great danger existed in the country; that there had been disclosed in the country a spirit which was incompatible with the constitution of the kingdom - that it threatened the destruction of all those rights which were most valuable - and that it aimed not only at the change of all
5   those political institutions which had hitherto constituted the pride and security of the country, but also at the subversion of property, and of course of all those rights on which society depended, which, if not speedily checked, was calculated to overthrow the principles upon which the property and happiness of society rested.[2]

The attitude of the Tory government was understandable: they had a responsibility to maintain public order. But their reactions had all the hallmarks of a party firmly intent on protecting the propertied classes and repelling demands for further reform. The Six Acts, passed in 1819, were further evidence of their determination to constrain radical activity. These imposed taxes on cheap newspapers, restricted the right of public meetings and increased the penalties for seditious libel.

Throughout this period, the Whigs' attitude towards reform was very disappointing. They were the one party which might have given credibility to the radical platform, but few Whigs expressed any genuine interest. The unrest in Britain between 1815 and 1820 alarmed them as much as the Tories. Grey, who led the party in the Commons, was anxious to preserve the pre-eminence of the landed class; like the Tories, many in his party profited from an undemocratic system of representation.

In practical terms, the reform movement had made no progress by 1820. Both Tories and Whigs had resisted reform, convinced that democracy was a dangerous concept. Their attitudes were still fundamentally shaped by the inherent belief that property had to be protected. It was the chief means of safeguarding the constitution.

2 1821-48: the Consolidation of Middle-Class Politics

Between 1821 and 1848 there were significant developments regarding attitudes towards parliamentary reform. These were most clearly demonstrated during two phases of agitation: the campaign for reform between 1830 and 1832, and the Chartist movement, 1836-48. During the first phase, a more responsive and less defensive attitude towards political change was evident amongst some politicians, most notably the Whigs. In addition, a more widespread grass-roots radical political platform emerged which, for the first time, united middle-class and working-class reformers in a concerted effort to gain franchise reform between 1830 and 1832. Yet having admitted the middle classes to the franchise in 1832, both Tories and Whigs were determined to oppose further democracy. These attitudes were likewise shared by the increasingly prominent middle classes who did not wish to see their newly acquired political and economic strengths undermined. The failure to obtain a working-class franchise in 1832 led to the second phase of agitation. Owing to its almost exclusively working-class membership, the Chartist movement met with predictable failure.

a) The Campaign for Reform, 1821-32

i) The Background to the Reform Crisis

Once the problems of war and the threat of revolution receded after 1822, a more constructive Tory administration prevailed, influenced by politicians such as the Home Secretary, Robert Peel, and the Foreign Secretary, Lord Canning. During this period the Tory Government embarked on trade policies which promoted free trade, thereby contributing towards long-term economic recovery. But the death of Lord Liverpool in 1828 revealed serious rifts within the party especially on the issues of Catholic emancipation and parliamentary reform.

During the 1820s, an unprecedented campaign in Ireland led by

Daniel O'Connell had challenged the discrimination against Catholics imposed by the Test and Corporation Acts. The campaign culminated in O'Connell's successful, although illegal, election as the MP for County Clare in 1828. Faced with the risk of escalating violence in Ireland if they continued to deny Catholics full civil rights, the Tories were forced to concede Catholic emancipation in 1829. This granted Catholics the right to hold public office, although the franchise qualification was redefined, eliminating the 40 shilling free-hold franchise and replacing it with a highly restrictive ten pound householder franchise. The act merely exacerbated the tensions within the party, with traditionalists viewing it as a betrayal of the important relationship between State and Anglican Church. This resistance to change was further evident in 1830 when the issue of parliamentary reform was revived.

In 1830, George IV, who had opposed both Catholic emancipation and parliamentary reform, died. His death necessitated a general election during which arguments in favour of reform became more prominent. This coincided with important developments in France where a peaceful, constitutional revolution had taken place, demon-strating that political change could occur without violence. Although Wellington was returned to power, his ill-advised comment in November 1830 that 'the Legislature and the system of representation possessed the full and entire confidence of the country'[3] signified a party increasingly out of touch with the wishes of the people. His subsequent defeat in the Commons led to the new king, William IV, summoning a Whig ministry under the leadership of Lord Grey.

ii) The Reform Crisis, 1830-2

What were the factors which encouraged the Whigs to enact the first major legislation on parliamentary reform in 1832? Their decision was part of a long-term process of change. As seen in Chapter 2, the transformation of Britain's political and economic structure had commenced, with the forces of the Industrial Revolution profoundly influencing attitudes and expectations. Britain needed its middle-class entrepreneurs to secure future prosperity. The governing classes could no longer remain so exclusively narrow-based.

Short-term factors also convinced the incoming Whigs that parlia-mentary reform was a priority. First, the successful Catholic emanci-pation campaign alerted them to the potential effectiveness of extra-parliamentary activity and the dangers of neglecting radical opinion. Secondly, large industrial towns now sought to secure their identity through direct representation. The new urban bourgeoisie was to be a key factor in persuading the Whigs to contemplate reform. This consensus for reform prompted Thomas Attwood, a Birmingham banker, to establish the Birmingham Political Union (BPU) in 1830 with the express intention of mobilising the middle and working classes in a concerted campaign for reform. Now a viable rationale for reform, such as that propounded by James Mill (see pages 23-24), had a broad base of support. During the next two years, Attwood's political unions achieved an unprecedented level of agitation. Yet the movement remained law-abiding, concentrating on peaceful tactics, conscious that violence would alienate middle-class allies. Thirdly, economic factors persuaded the Whigs that to ignore reform might be dangerous. In 1830, a severe economic depression caused widespread unrest, especially in agricultural areas where the notorious 'Swing Riots' served as a reminder of the dangers of 'mob' protest.

The Whigs' decision to introduce a reform bill in March 1831 instigated a serious political crisis in Britain because forces of reaction were locked in confrontation with radicalism. The former, as exemplified by the Tories, demonstrated an innate fear of greater parliamentary representation. The existing system guaranteed the security of the constitution, as well as Britain's traditional institutions - the monarchy and the Church. Underlying their opposition was a natural dread of losing their aristocratic monopoly of power and all their privileges (see pages 7-9). As this satirical cartoon on page 40, published just after the defeat of the first Reform Bill in April 1831, reveals, the Tories were perceived by their critics to be clinging desperately to the old vestiges of power. The Tories had one advantage, however. They possessed a natural majority in the House of Lords and could use this to defeat the proposals passed by the Commons. Their intransigent opposition to reform merely provoked wide-range popular protest.

The Whigs had several clear objectives. Their most important aim was to preserve aristocratic influence and property. But in a perceptive move, the Whigs hoped to satisfy the industrial middle classes by granting them the franchise. In a speech to the House of Commons in March 1832, the great Whig supporter of the Reform Bill, Thomas Macaulay, outlined some of the problems which the current, defective Parliament had failed to remedy:

1   The distress which the country had suffered, and of which it had so bitterly complained, he must attribute to an unthrifty squandering of the public money ... - to the negligence of that House - to defects in the Representative system, which had made the House more the council of
5   the Government than the defender of the people - to laws deservedly unpopular, ... - to laws made for the benefit of particular classes at the expense of the people generally - in short, he attributed the distress to Ministers who had not yet been controlled by Parliament, and to Parliament who had not before its eyes the fear of the people.[4]

These were the very protests which had figured so forcefully since the 1780s of exploitation by an unrepresentative Parliament. The fact that the Whigs conceived the practicality of addressing some of these grievances revealed the extent to which Whig attitudes had progressed since the late eighteenth century.

The Balance of Power, *May 1831. The Whigs sit on the right whilst the Tories are on the left. The Devil stands with a placard labelled 'Reform'.*

iii) The Effects of the Reform Act, 1832

The Reform Act was poor compensation for those seeking dramatic change in the system of representation. Although one in five males in England and Wales, one in eight in Scotland and one in 20 in Ireland were eligible to vote, huge discrepancies existed nationally regarding who was enfranchised. The principle of owning property as a pre-requisite for voting remained, and with a huge range of property values applying, there was little consistency in who got the vote.

Nor was there any significant change in the composition of Parliament. The 1832 Reform Act was not intended as a progressive piece of legislation: hence the dominance of the aristocracy prevailed, both within executive government - the Cabinet and ministerial posts - and in the legislative chamber of the Commons.

But in the long term, 1832 was of singular importance. It compelled political parties to seek the potential vote of the new electorate, the middle classes who, if they owned property worth £10 per annum, could now vote. For the immediate future, their main interests rested in local affairs such as local government (see page 44), health and education, but a vital partnership had been forged between the landed classes and the industrial middle classes. It was a formidable alliance, based on the premise of liberal ideals, which secured polit-ical stability, and an absence of serious political strife.

For the working class, their exclusion was a bitter setback, not least because they could have little impact in determining the subsequent evolution of democracy. In this respect, the Painite tradition had received a fatal blow, whilst that of Mill and Bentham was in the ascen-dancy. The implications of this anti-democratic measure were signifi-cant. The middle classes now had the political power to underpin the capitalist system and determine the future framework of democracy in Britain. (For more details on the passage of the 1832 legislation, see Robert Pearce and Roger Stearn, *Government and Reform 1815-1918*, Hodder & Stoughton, *Access to History*, 1994, Chapter 3; and Duncan Watts, *Whigs, Radicals and Liberals 1815-1914*, Hodder & Stoughton *Access to History*, 1995, Chapter 3.)

b) The Demise of Popular Radicalism, 1832-48

i) Chartism

In the aftermath of 1832, the last of the truly nineteenth-century working-class protest movements, Chartism, emerged, providing an unprecedented channel for working-class demands. The old rhetoric which attacked an unreformed parliament, despotism and corruption and which called for a restored constitution now included more pressing grievances shaped by the effects of *laissez-faire* economics and capitalism. On a wider scale, long working hours and the harsh reali-ties of the Poor Law Amendment Act contributed to a strong sense of frustration and a compelling belief that the manufacturing bosses were exploiting the working class. Added to this recipe for dissent was the political betrayal by the Whigs in 1832. As a result, Chartists viewed themselves as victims of class legislation. Their solution was to submit a radical programme which advocated greater democratic control.

What was the nature of Chartist democracy? Although Chartism reiterated the very same six demands put forward by the Westminster Association in 1780 (see page 34), it embraced a more comprehensive understanding of democracy. Firstly, its wide appeal made it the first national working-class movement. Secondly, it sought to realise democracy by endeavouring to establish a People's Parliament in 1839 on the grounds that the existing Parliament was unrepresentative. The contemporary engraving of the National Convention on the 4 February 1839 (see page 43) depicts an occasion of great solemnity, as delegates from across the country gathered to implement direct representation of the people. These men would scarcely seem the dangerous demagogues whose democratic ideals seemingly alarmed the ruling classes so much. Thirdly, Chartism was an inclusive movement, one which went way beyond political aims to embrace religion, education and land reform. As Eileen Yeo commented:

> The very way in which the Chartists tried to govern their movement disclosed a blueprint for collective control which involved much more than periodic voting for Parliament.[5]

The fears that Chartism would undermine the Constitution were strongly denied by one of the main leaders of the movement, William Lovett:

1   The supposition that Universal Suffrage would give the working classes a *preponderating power* in the House of Commons, is not borne out by the experience of other countries. They are far from possessing such a power even in America, where wealth and rank have far less influence
5   than with us, and where the exercise of the suffrage for more than half a century have given them opportunities to get their rights better represented than they are. But *wealth* with them, as with us, will always maintain *an undue influence*, till the people are *morally* and *politically* instructed ... But the great advantages of the suffrage in the interim will
10   be these: it will afford the people general and superior *means* of instruction; it will awaken and concentrate human intellect to remove the evils of social life; and will compel the representatives of the people to redress grievances, improve laws, and provide means of happiness in proportion to the enlightened desires of public opinion. Such indeed are
15   the results we anticipate from the passing of the PEOPLE'S CHARTER.[6]

The failure of Chartism in 1848 indicated several key factors about the premature nature of its democratic goals. The movement stood little chance of success whilst the government remained so unwilling to make concessions. The derision amongst members of the ruling

The National Convention, 4 February 1839

class which greeted Chartism's collapse reflected the continuing lack of respect for working-class movements. This was compounded by the fragmentation within Chartism which detracted from its credibility. Finally, the demise of Chartism was yet further proof that without the co-operation of the middle classes, the principle of universal suffrage was an illusory goal.

ii) The Impact of the Middle-Class Franchise

In the aftermath of 1832, subtle but perceptible changes occurred in mainstream politics. The Tories were encouraged to re-evaluate their political policies and principles, most notably under their new leader, Robert Peel, who replaced Wellington in 1832. It was Peel's incisive leadership which forced the Conservative Party, as it came to be known, to confront some stark choices: either to maintain the principles of High or Ultra Toryism - narrow self-interest, support for the landed classes and resistance to reform - or to adopt a more pragmatic and conciliatory approach to politics, one which sympathised with the interests of the expanding industrial middle classes. Peel's realisation that political survival depended on presenting a more moderate face of conservatism was publicised in his famous Tamworth Manifesto, 1834. This document was both forward-looking and traditional in its themes, promising a 'careful review of institutions, civil and ecclesiastical' and 'the correction of proved abuses and the redress of real grievances'. Peel appreciated that political reform was a reality but he remained adamant that 1832 was not a progressive piece of legislation.

1   With respect to the Reform Bill itself, I will repeat now the declaration
     which I made when I entered the House of Commons as a Member of
     the Reformed Parliament, that I consider the Reform Bill a final and
     irrevocable settlement of a great constitutional question - a settlement
5   which no friend to the peace and welfare of this country would attempt
     to disturb, either by direct or by insidious means.[7]

Peel's contributions to creating a more caring face of Conservatism had important long-term implications, in particular with respect to attitudes towards the people. Unfortunately Peel was unable to unite his party. Divisions over free trade were deep-rooted, with Benjamin Disraeli proclaiming the alternative merits of Protectionism. Following Peel's defeat in 1846 and his subsequent death in 1850, the Conservative Party did not regain a majority in the House of Commons until 1874.

Having gained office in 1831, the Whigs remained in power until defeated by Peel in 1841. Following the 1832 Reform Act, the Whigs concentrated on administrative reforms, which often reflected the Benthamite concept of increasing government efficiency, as well as social and economic improvements. One act which sought to improve local administration was the Municipal Corporations Act, 1835. This act introduced the concept of local accountability by creating locally elected councils. A third of local council members were to be elected annually by ratepayers with a three year residency. The act reflected the contemporary importance attached to local politics, especially by the industrial middle classes. In the long term, the act was significant because local political power became a stepping stone to acquiring more national political power.

3 The Emergence of a Liberal Democracy, 1849-68

In 1866, the Liberals introduced a second reform bill. The defeat of this bill, and the subsequent success of the Conservatives in guiding an even more radical bill through Parliament, signified a notable watershed in the development of democracy in Britain. How had attitudes changed, therefore, between 1849 and 1866 and what were the factors which facilitated the resurgence of interest in political reform?

a) The Changing Climate of Opinion

Between 1846, when Peel was defeated, and 1866, the Whigs and their successors, the Liberals, dominated British politics. Throughout this period, aristocratic government survived because the middle classes did not yet possess the momentum to challenge the monopoly of the ruling class. The influence of Lord Palmerston, Whig/Liberal prime minister in 1855-8 and 1859-65, was also a deterrent to parliamentary reform. Palmerston focused on promoting British foreign policy, whilst at home his ministries were characterised by minimum government interference, respect for the dignity of the constitution and the maintenance of a system in which people accepted their position in society. Palmerston vehemently opposed any suggestion that the existence of corruption and bribery, inequality of representation or the continued domination of government by the landed classes signified a deficiency in the parliamentary system.

Nevertheless, these conservative attitudes were gradually eroded by changing political and economic circumstances. One contributory factor was the political realignment which occurred during the late 1840s and 1850s. Peelites, moderate Whigs, Dissenters and Radicals increasingly shared common political goals, the result being the emergence of a new political party - the Liberals - in 1859. The tenets of the Liberal Party were to echo much of the political philosophy of J.S. Mill and Walter Bagehot, not least the belief that a careful review of parliamentary institutions was now imperative. Thus the Liberal Party became the main exponent of liberalism, although adherents to that philosophy still transcended party divides.

The impact of middle-class reformers on the Liberals was also important. Leading campaigners such as John Bright and Richard Cobden, founders in 1849 of the Parliamentary Financial Reform League which agitated for tax reduction and extension of the franchise, added respectability to the cause of reform. Bright argued persuasively that reform would consolidate the forces of capitalism. Those who had worked hard to secure the success of capitalism - the working classes - had demonstrated their trustworthiness to exercise the vote and should be rewarded.

The death of Palmerston in 1865 was instrumental in releasing previously latent demands for reform. His successor was Earl Russell, but it was his chancellor of the exchequer, William Gladstone, who now acquired the reputation as an advocate of popular reform. Gladstone never abandoned his long-held belief that the aristocracy were the natural rulers, but he became convinced that the working classes were morally entitled to the vote. In 1864, Gladstone's decision to champion the rights of the working class helped to bring the reform movement back onto the political agenda. He defined his criteria for enfranchising the working classes.

1 What are the qualities which fit a man for the exercise of a privilege such as the franchise? Self-command, self-control, respect for order, patience under suffering, confidence in the law, regard for superiors; and when, I should like to ask, were all these great qualities exhibited in a
5 manner more signal,... than under the profound affliction of the winter of 1862?[8]

Gladstone had been impressed by the stoic fortitude of Lancashire cotton workers who had withstood severe economic deprivation during the winter of 1862 because of the American Civil War. Despite the prospect of famine, they had not engaged in violent protest. Consequently Gladstone believed that their self-restraint and strength of character demonstrated their reliability to vote. He was convinced that the enfranchisement of the urban working class would not upset the equilibrium of the country. Hence, in 1866, he instigated proposals for parliamentary reform. Previous reform bills had been submitted at intervals to Parliament, but now there was a more positive climate of opinion.

The Conservatives had also undergone some significant changes in attitude by 1866. During the first half of the nineteenth century, the Tories had adamantly defended the *status quo*, on the grounds that any concession to the disenfranchised would jeopardise the security of the constitution. But admitting the middle classes to the franchise had not destabilised the constitution as they anticipated. Thus some Conservatives, including the leader, Lord Derby, and Benjamin Disraeli, who led the party in the Commons, were ready to make further concessions on the grounds that it was now safe to grant the franchise to urban householders.

b) The Passing of the Second Reform Act, 1867

In 1866, Lord Russell's government introduced proposals for a reform bill. As leader of the party in the House of Commons, Gladstone dominated the debates. The intention was to enfranchise all borough householders paying £7 a year in rent, and in the counties all householders with or without land paying £14 in rent. The rationale was that limited reform would benefit the skilled and trustworthy members of the working class, but exclude the uneducated and therefore politically unreliable members of the lower stratum of society. About half the adult male population would have received the vote.

Opposition came from two quarters. Right-wing Liberals, led by Robert Lowe, argued that greater democracy was an exceedingly dangerous concept. He envisaged a dramatic decline in the character of Parliament, tainted by people whose only objective would be their own self-interest. Good government would be undermined by uneducated and corrupt individuals, and Britain would sink to the level of the worst kind of democracy, as exemplified by the assemblies in North America.

For the Conservatives, Lowe's attacks on Gladstone were most welcome. Derby and Disraeli quickly realised that an 'unholy' alliance with these dissident Liberals could help them attain a previously tenuous goal: government office. In June 1866, a successful opposition amendment to the bill was passed, forcing the Liberals to resign.

Derby and Disraeli then formed a minority government and were responsible in March 1867 for introducing their own reform bill.

During the subsequent months, the government and the opposition engaged in intense debates, during which the Conservatives granted several radical amendments that expanded the criteria for the franchise. Consequently the final act was far more liberal than previously intended (see page 14). Why did the Conservatives permit such concessions?

One factor which merits examination is the extent to which the Conservatives were influenced by external pressure. An active campaign was waged by two reform groups: the essentially working-class Reform League, led by Edmund Beales, and the more middle-class Reform Union, led by John Bright. Yet even the League had modest ambitions, namely universal manhood suffrage based on household suffrage and a lodger franchise. Moreover, the very lowest orders of the working class would remain disenfranchised due to their inability to meet the one year residency qualification for voting. The middle-class reformers accommodated the principle of limited working-class enfranchisement on the grounds that those demonstrating respectability and responsibility had proven their worthiness of the vote.

Both organisations campaigned for reform against the background of heightened social and economic distress caused by harsh winter conditions, an economic slump and a cholera epidemic. John Bright warned that to deny reform would exacerbate the threat of public disorder. On 6 May 1867 a large-scale meeting was held in Hyde Park to demand reform. Despite back-up support from at least 10,000 police and military, the government was forced to abandon its efforts to ban the meeting on the grounds that it would be impossible to disperse a crowd of 100,000. It was a serious humiliation for the government in that they were seen to have permitted a blatant defiance of the law and to have encouraged working-class solidarity. The fact that significant concessions were made to the proposed reform bill shortly thereafter certainly suggests that external pressures were instrumental in affecting government opinion.

The other factor frequently analysed is the precise role of Disraeli during the debates. Why did he resist amendments proposed by Gladstone, which would have limited the franchise, but accept, often with little debate, other, more extreme amendments? It appeared that he was determined to thwart Gladstone and to retain the initiative within the Commons at all costs. Was this the action of a pure opportunist, manipulating the Commons for his own political gain, or was he swayed by the external agitation? Maurice Cowling claimed that Disraeli permitted such a large expansion of the electorate because he was engaged in a cynical game of political manoeuvring, designed to retain office and 'dish Gladstone'. Yet this viewpoint ignores the perspective proffered by Royden Harrison and Clive Behagg that

Disraeli was compelled to grant concessions because of the external pressures for reform. Bruce Coleman concluded in one article that:

1 traditionalist Conservatives like Disraeli and Salisbury feared that merely negative and confrontational responses to the new forces in the political nation would drive them into the arms of the Liberals and promote further radicalism. Prudent Tories should provide their own
5 version of 'democratic' policies to prevent worse.[9]

c) The 1867 Reform Act

As a result of the 1867 Reform Act, a third of the adult male population could vote, although women were still excluded. The Act set the scene for the future development of mass politics, both in terms of representation and the behaviour of political parties which would soon appreciate the merits of cultivating the working-class vote. Modern party political organisation was an inevitable consequence of expanding the franchise. The working class acquired some political kudos as politicians sought their vote.

For the immediate future, however, the 1867 Reform Act was not regarded as the precursor to full democracy. It did not enfranchise the lower strata of society because only men of property received the vote. Nor did it confront the problems of corruption at elections and the lack of a secret ballot. Redistribution of seats consolidated Conservative electoral interests in the counties, although the Liberals were set to maintain their advantage in the boroughs. As yet, few people envisaged working-class MPs, but the mould of traditional nineteenth-century politics was poised to break as the Liberals in particular moved towards a more radical programme of politics. (For more details of the Second Reform Act, 1867, see Pearce and Stearn, *Government and Reform*, Chapter 4.)

4 Conclusion

The changing relationship between government and the people had important implications for the growth of democracy in Britain. Yet was this development, as Macaulay had argued, due purely to the actions of wise rulers, or was the process of change more complex? If there was a consensus in 1867 that the urban working class should be enfranchised, surely that consensus was the result of a wealth of different causal factors.

Changing government attitudes towards the people were central to the emergence of democracy. The concern to retain oligarchical rule had been replaced by the realisation that moderate political reform would ensure stability and the continuation of parliamentary government. For the Tories, the acceptance of pragmatic politics came slowly. As seen in their reactions to events between the 1780s and the

1830s, their desire to adhere to the principles of aristocratic rule was tenacious. Fear of 'the people', aggravated by the fate of the landowners in France during the Revolution, impeded the adoption of more caring policies. But although more humanitarian policies ensued, the Conservatives still believed in traditional government. This involved, for many Conservatives, the preservation of the paternalistic values of a pre-industrial society. Even if it did make political common sense to enfranchise the urban working class, that did not lessen the importance of retaining the dominance of Britain's natural ruling elite. Subsequent policies (see Chapter 5) were implemented with the prime intention of keeping the working man in his rightful place in society, despite his ability to vote.

The Whigs and Liberals accepted the need for political reform more easily. Unlike the Tories, they were less restrained by traditional dogma, although disunity within the party certainly impeded the early emergence of reforming policies. Nevertheless, the Whigs developed a strong affinity with the rising middle classes, and so were quicker to appreciate the electoral advantage of extending the franchise. Whigs and Liberals were more comfortable with the tenets of capitalism and so they were quicker to encourage the spirit of individualism and the development of entrepreneurial skills. It therefore seemed logical that those who contributed to the successful expansion of the British economy should eventually be rewarded with the vote.

But the expansion of the franchise was not just the result of 'enlightened' government policies. The climate of opinion would not have advanced so far without the important ongoing radical debate. Political aims were clearly articulated, and ideas were underpinned by a range of radical political writing which espoused the concepts of liberalism. Likewise, although interpretations differ as to the degree of influence exerted by the people on governments, it is surely the case that mass pressure was instrumental in breaking down the barriers to reform. Talk of 'democracy' may have alarmed the authorities, and in many cases determined their response to political agitation, but ultimately they accepted that greater democracy was not intrinsically dangerous. By 1867, the threat of 'mass pressure' with its accompanying violence had receded, to be replaced by moderate working-class lobbying. Although working-class activity alone could not gain any political concessions, once the middle classes recognised the respectability of the working classes, a strong alliance emerged which was undoubtedly a major factor in persuading politicians to expand the franchise in 1867.

The progress of democracy in Britain was not only secured by political change. Full democracy could only develop within the context of greater civil and religious liberties, as well as economic prosperity. Greater tolerance of Dissenters and Catholics was an essential factor in facilitating the gradual erosion of traditional, aristocratic government. In addition, the growing ability of labour to organise itself had significant long-term implications for the future of democracy. With the repeal of the Combination Acts in 1825, a precedent was set for the legality of trade unions. Just as Chartists and their radical predecessors considered working-class political representation as a means of rectifying economic injustices, so trade unionists eventually saw the advantage of getting working-class candidates into Parliament. Finally, a considerable percentage of the population saw material improvements in their standard of living as the result of *laissez-faire* economics, with the middle classes and skilled workers the chief beneficiaries. Economic stability was a natural corollary to political stability.

Yet despite these achievements, were opportunities lost in 1867? In one respect, working-class aspirations had been tamed by the combined effects of social and economic stability, and consequently the radical political movement lost its militancy. Despite Marx's prediction that the exploitation of the working class in Britain's industrial cities would lead to the first revolution of the proletariat and the overthrow of the bourgeoisie, Britain avoided revolution. There was little scope in Britain for Marxism to flourish because, compared with many European countries, there was a notable lack of class conflict within the country. What would have been the outcome if the working-class movement had been more militant and retained some of the dynamism of the earlier reform campaigns? Compared with France, where all adult males had the vote after 1848, and Prussia, where Bismarck granted a national suffrage to all males in 1867, Britain still possessed a very limited franchise. Despite the significance of the Second Reform Act in advancing greater representation, was the absence of a secret ballot and the failure to reform parliamentary boundaries, plus the continued neglect of female suffrage, an indication that in reality, true democracy still had a long way to go?

References
1 T. Wooler (ed), *The Black Dwarf*, vol.3 no.30, 28 July 1819, p.487.
2 *Hansard's Parliamentary Debates*, vol.XLI, 29 November 1819, col.380-1.
3 *Hansard's Parliamentary Debates*, 3rd Series, vol.I, 2 November 1830, col.52-3.
4 *Hansard's Parliamentary Debates*, 3rd Series, vol.XI, 19 March 1832, col.455-6.
5 Eileen Yeo, 'Some Practices and Problems of Chartist Democracy', in D. Thompson and James Epstein (eds), *The Chartist Experience: Studies in Working-Class Radicalism and Cultures, 1830 - 60* (Macmillan Press, 1982), p.374.
6 W. Lovett and J. Collins, *Chartism - a new organization of the People* (Leicester, 1969), p.13.
7 Sir Robert Peel, *Address to the Electors of the Borough of Tamworth*, December 1834 (Roake and Varty, 1835), p.4.
8 *Hansard's Parliamentary Debates*, 3rd Series, vol.CLXXV, 11 May 1864, col.324-5.

9   Bruce Coleman 'Tory Democracy under Disraeli and Salisbury', *Modern History Review*,1990, vol.1 no.4, (April)p.29.

Answering essay questions on 'Government and the People, 1780-1868'

Questions on parliamentary reform often focus on key developments such as the 1832 or 1867 Reform Acts. But it is also important to be able to look beyond the legislation itself and to analyse the context in which reform was either successful or unsuccessful.

1. Account for the failure of the parliamentary reform movement in Britain prior to 1830.

2. Why was it possible to grant the urban working class the franchise in 1867 but not in 1832?

3. To what extent did the effects of the 1832 Reform Act warrant the excitement aroused in its passing?

4. 'By 1867, pragmatism had replaced dogma in British politics'. Discuss.

As you write your essay, it is very important to refer frequently to your essay plan, especially as you write the middle section in which your main ideas are developed. It is at this stage that students tend to digress from answering the question. If you have successfully listed all the key points of your argument in your plan, writing the main section should not be difficult. Bear in mind that you have to develop an overall argument in which each paragraph will provide supporting ideas and evidence.

The purpose of each paragraph is to discuss one issue in detail. Set out the main point of the paragraph in its opening sentence, and then deploy relevant evidence to support that point. If, as in question 1, you are asked to explain the reasons for certain developments, make sure that the paragraph is directed towards that explanation. This is where analysis rather than description is so important. For example, in question 1, there will be a wide range of reasons for the failure of the parliamentary reform movement prior to 1830. You should avoid describing just what happened up until 1830, with only a brief comment of explanation in the conclusion. Instead, consider what types of reasons caused the failure: long-term, short-term, political, economic, social. Which were the most important reasons - political attitudes, the effects of the French Revolution, lack of middle-class support? Each paragraph will then seek to prove a particular point, backed up by the appropriate evidence. Finally, remember that your paragraphs must be considered as part of a coherent whole. Ensuring a logical transition from one paragraph to another is very important, so that one can gain a sense of an argument progressing towards a logical conclusion.

Source-based questions on 'Government and the People, 1780-1868'

1. The issue of reform, 1819

Read the two extracts from *The Black Dwarf* and *Hansard's Parliamentary Debates* on page 36. Answer the following questions.

a) In the extract from *The Black Dwarf*, what does the author mean by 'oppression' and 'despotism' (line 6)? (2 marks)

b) According to the report in *The Black Dwarf*, why did the reformers in Leeds assume that political reform would 'save the trading and labouring classes from ruin' (lines 10-11)? (4 marks)

c) What does Lord Castlereagh's reference to a 'great danger existed in the country' (line 1) reveal about Tory attitudes towards the reform movement? (6 marks)

d) Both documents refer to the 'constitution'. How and why do the two interpretations of the 'constitution' differ? (8 marks)

2. Chartism

Read the speech by William Lovett on page 42 and study the engraving of the National Convention on page 43. Answer the following questions.

a) Why did Lovett feel that it was necessary for the people to receive moral and political instruction (lines 8-9)? (3 marks)

b) Why did Lovett emphasise that universal suffrage would not give the working classes undue influence in the Commons? (4 marks)

c) What image of the Chartist movement does the engraving of the National Convention convey? (5 marks)

d) What are the strengths and limitations of this engraving as historical evidence of that meeting? (8 marks)

Hints and advice: Interpreting historical documents can be quite straightforward, provided that you are methodical. You will frequently encounter unfamiliar language and phrases which, on a first reading, may be difficult to understand. You should read through each extract several times, slowly and carefully in order to grasp the overall meaning. Your own historical knowledge will also help you to appreciate the context in which the source was written. For example, an understanding of the historical events which preceded the Peterloo Massacre of 1819 will facilitate your ability to interpret the main points of the extract from *The Black Dwarf*. You should also try to determine what is the aim of the document. Who is the intended audience? Is the author seeking to justify certain actions, convey a certain opinion, or win support for a particular viewpoint?

Question 2a is a straightforward test of comprehension. The main thrust of Lovett's argument is that the people should receive specific education. Your task is to interpret his reasons, and to explain them in your own words. Do not assume that the answer is contained within just one sentence. You should look beyond the obvious explanation for more subtle reasons.

Question 2b requires skilful deployment of historical knowledge. What, for example, had been the main fear of the ruling classes ever since the French Revolution? You need to comment on existing attitudes towards 'democracy' in order to appreciate Lovett's motives. What was he trying to prove and whom was he trying to reassure?

Question 2c first requires you to analyse the images of the Chartists conveyed in the engraving. Taking the picture at face-value, you can draw some obvious conclusions about the types of people attending the meeting. Note their dress and the room where they are convening. However, you should also consider whether the image of respectability is significant or not. What does this imply about the nature of the Chartist movement?

Question 2d is a familiar question in exam papers. How useful or reliable is a document as historical evidence? Knowing who produced the source can be important; but in the case of this engraving, the artist is unknown. Nevertheless, what can you infer from his choice of subject material? Why did the artist record this meeting? Do you think that he supported or opposed the Chartists? The limitations of the source may be less obvious. Be ready to question whether the artist was accurate, or whether his images were typical of the Chartists as a whole. What further information would you need to verify his portrayal?

Summary Diagram
Government and the People, 1780-1868

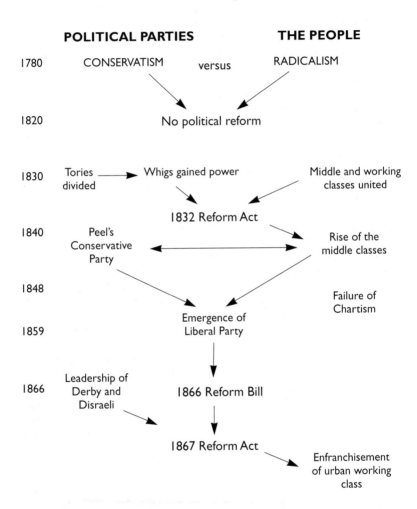

4 The Growth of Party Politics, 1868-1906

The 1867 Reform Act had both significant long-term and short-term effects. It confirmed the trend in British politics towards parliamentary government, whilst still preventing the adoption of full democracy. It consolidated the authority of the middle classes as key participants in government, but also revealed the many inconsistencies in the existing political system.

The expansion of the franchise to just the urban working class was one inconsistency. Remember that in the boroughs, all male householders with a 12-month residency and lodgers paying £10 per annum in rent could now vote. Thus the exclusion of the agricultural workers seemed to many observers an anomaly which should be rectified by equalising the qualifications to vote. Likewise, the management of elections appeared increasingly outmoded in the age of greater democracy. The right to vote independently and to conduct elections immune from bribery and corruption were central issues after 1867. All three were addressed by 1885.

These achievements in electoral reform had important implications for the conduct of politics in the late nineteenth century. First, politicians had to accept the reality of a more democratic society which expected a greater degree of accountability by government towards the voters. Given those conditions, relevant policies had to be devised so that each party could take advantage of the new democracy, capture votes and gain the powers of government.

The second major effect was that parties had to reform their political organisations in order to win the minds of the electorate. Hitherto, they had relied on voluntary help to manage election campaigns and gain support. This task was now too demanding to be left to individual goodwill. As a result, both Liberals and Conservatives built up efficient, professional party structures, with a nationwide network of local party organisations. The political education of the public became an extensive activity as each party competed for the minds and hearts of the electorate. In this respect, the modern political age was born.

1 Political Reform, 1868-85

The 1867 Reform Act had granted a much wider franchise than most politicians intended. Faced with an increased electorate, greater pressure now prevailed to reform and modernise electoral practices. Eventually, politicians also conceded the need to establish a more equitable franchise.

a) The Ballot Act, 1872

The first, the Ballot Act of 1872 (see the table on page 57), sought to counteract the escalating costs of fighting elections as well as the chaos of the hustings, where bribery and corruption of voters continued unabated. Reformers argued that landlords exerted undue pressure on tenants to vote for a favoured candidate and criticised the lengths to which candidates would go in order to bring their supporters to the hustings. In the attack below on the Conservative candidate W.H. Smith at the election of 1868, you should note the reference to Smith's 'well fed workmen' who have clearly been encouraged to parade through the streets in support of their employer. If voters could vote in secrecy, placing their vote in a ballot box, such corruption would cease. Opponents understandably feared the impact of a secret ballot. Landlords expected tenants to support the landlord's political party. Voter independence would undermine their influence.

In 1872, however, the Liberals bowed to the pressures for reform. The Act was significant because it accelerated the demise of patronage in British politics. The removal of patronage was an essential prerequisite to the establishment of democracy.

b) The Corrupt and Illegal Practices (Prevention) Act, 1883

Yet the failure of the Ballot Act to eliminate corruption necessitated further reform in 1883. In the counties, local landlords still influenced voting choices whilst in the boroughs, powerful employers, such as the Ferguson family in Carlisle, expected their political alle-

A newspaper cartoon, 21 November 1868

giances to be endorsed by their workmen. The influence of the local employer was often so pervasive that the candidate would have little need to canvass.

Nevertheless, rowdier elements of the electorate quickly appreciated that they could sell their vote to the highest bidder. Riots, election violence, bribery and corruption remained familiar features of elections, not least the election of 1880 during which election expenses reached alarming levels. This prompted calls for government intervention. With resources strained by the demands of canvassing a wider electorate, both Conservatives and Liberals recognised the potential benefits of legislation to curb corruption. Politics had to adapt to the new era of the mass voter. Ensuring that elections were conducted in an orderly and manageable fashion was one logical step.

The Corrupt Practices and Illegal Practices (Prevention) Act of 1883 was a vital ingredient in the growth of democracy in Britain. Political practice had gained a new code of ethics. Centuries of tradition had been finally undermined.

c) The Third Reform Act, 1884-5

The Second Reform Act had accelerated the process of government by direct consent, and this in turn enhanced the concept that political power should reside in the community. To many liberal-minded

---

Political Reform 1868-85

The Ballot Act, 1872
Voters voted in voting booths, placing votes in a ballot box. Election officials counted the votes.

Corrupt and Illegal Practices Act, 1883
Limited candidates' election expenses according to size of electorate. Imposed fines and imprisonment for violation of the law.

Third Reform Act, 1884
In the counties, householders and £10 lodgers gained the vote. A £10 occupier franchise was created for those living in shops or offices. A uniform franchise for both counties and boroughs now operated. The electorate increased by 2 million.

Redistribution of Seats Act, 1885
Boroughs with fewer than 15,000 lost both their MPs, those with less than 50,000 people lost one MP. 142 seats were redistributed. Most constituencies were now single-member only. Equal-sized constituencies now existed in most seats. English Boundary Commission set up to redraw boundaries. Distinct rural and urban constituencies created.

people, the extension of the franchise to rural workers would be the natural corollary to 1867 and would complete unfinished business. In this respect, the Third Reform Act consolidated the initiatives of 1867.

Although the events surrounding the passage of the Third Reform Act were in no way as turbulent as in 1832 or 1867, the Liberals encountered several difficulties. Conservatives viewed the Liberal motives with great suspicion, claiming that they merely promoted enfranchisement of the agricultural workers for their own benefit. The Conservative, William Ansell Day, commented:

> 1 It is said the franchise has been extended to all householders in towns, and, therefore, it would be an act of injustice any longer to withhold it from householders in the country. This would be true if the franchise were a right and not a privilege; but no responsible politician would now
> 5 advocate that exploded dogma, and with it falls to the ground the argument of injustice....
>
> The men who demand it are not the working classes.... It is the men who hope to use the masses who urge that the suffrage should be conferred upon a numerous and ignorant class.[1]

In contrast, the Liberal view was that extension of the franchise would enhance the practice of government.

> 1 In the House of Commons all sections and interests should be represented, as is now the case with wealth, property, the highest intelligence, education, and wisdom; aristocratic, landed, law, literary, professional, scientific, official, and last, though not least, trading, commercial, & manu-
> 5 facturing interests. Every portion of the community should be similarly privileged, so as to obtain that vital force without which political life would stagnate. ... It is, therefore, of practical utility to the State; and should, undoubtedly, be granted to the agricultural labourers unless substantial proofs of its unwisdom can be produced against it.
> 10 ... The Middle Class (Artisan) was enfranchised because of its loyalty, judgement, and desire for, and interest in, stable government. Do not the County householders possess similar qualifications to recommend them?[2]

A second problem arose because the Conservatives made their support for an extension of the franchise conditional upon a redistribution of seats. This would counteract a possible increase in Liberal votes by adjusting constituency boundaries and allocation of seats in the Conservatives' favour. They therefore planned to obstruct the Franchise Bill in the House of Lords unless it was linked to a Redistribution Bill. The Liberals were furious that their efforts to keep the two acts separate were being thwarted by action which they claimed was undemocratic and which undermined the authority of the Commons. However, after protracted negotiations the Liberals acquiesced in a Redistribution Bill. The final outcome was the Third

Reform Act, although it comprised two separate acts: the Franchise Act (1884) and the Redistribution Act (1885).

The Franchise Act was significant because it endorsed the principle of a uniform franchise for both counties and boroughs. Representation took one more cautious step towards greater democracy although, with an increased electorate of approximately only two million, at least 40 per cent of the adult male population remained unenfranchised. The residence qualification excluded many working-class men whose transient work prevented them from remaining 12 months in one place. Adult men who lived with their parents and paid no rent were unenfranchised, as were members of the armed forces, or those on poor relief. Essentially, the poorer members of society were disadvantaged, not least because the principle of property still determined who could vote. A further negative feature of the act was the fact that the female franchise was totally neglected.

The Redistribution Act was equally important in modernising the British political system. The Conservatives reconciled themselves to reform, accepting that single-member constituencies enabled them to retain influence more easily in the county boroughs, whilst also making it easier for them to gain seats in middle-class urban areas. A number of safe Conservative seats in cities were created as a result of redistribution. The Liberals believed that they had successfully maintained their tradition of supporting political reform.

2 Party Politics

After 1868 both the Liberals and the Conservatives engaged in a review of party policies. Each party experienced factional divisions as different interests groups propounded their interpretations of Liberalism or Conservatism. This analysis and discussion of ideas was clearly driven by motives of pragmatism amd self-interest. Both parties realised the enormous potential of support created by the process of democratic reform. Having conceded enfranchisement, the parties competed for votes. As will be discussed in Section 3, party organisation would be crucial. But viable, attractive policies were also essential.

a) The Liberal Party

By 1867 liberalism was a firmly established political creed, having evolved from the writings of James Mill, Bentham, J.S. Mill and Bagehot. Several fundamental beliefs underpinned mid-nineteenth-century liberalism. The first was the principle of parliamentary government, albeit a limited democracy in which a minority group still held the reins of power. The second belief upheld individual liberty and the right to compete freely with others. Thirdly, there was an intrinsic faith in the merits of *laissez-faire* capitalism. With the emergence of the Liberal Party, these ideas formed the foundations of what came to be recognised as Gladstonian Liberalism. The question now facing the Liberal Party was whether these ideas were sufficiently flexible to adjust to the changing needs and expectations of society.

Yet, as the years of almost continuous Conservative Government between 1885 and 1906 testify, the Liberals were divided as to how they should appeal to the electorate. Four wide-ranging and often controversial approaches were explored during this period of opposition. The outcome saw the emergence of a liberal philosophy distinctly different from that of nineteenth-century Gladstonian Liberalism.

i) The response of Gladstone

Gladstone's first ministry, 1868-74, failed to develop a clear rapport with the new electorate. Despite several administrative reforms, its policies lacked democratic appeal and the new urban voters delivered their verdict in 1874. Defeat convinced many Liberals that the party would have to embrace new policies if they were to capture the support of the wider electorate.

Gladstone's solution was to rally his party around a single cause, in this case, the apparent immorality of Disraeli's foreign policy. During the 1880 election campaign, Gladstone toured Scotland denouncing 'Beaconsfieldism', named after Disraeli's title of Lord Beaconsfield, and castigating Disraeli's suppport for the Turks' persecution of Christians in Bulgaria. His 'Midlothian' campaign, so called after Gladstone's constituency, sought to re-establish a moral code of conduct in foreign policy. His fiery condemnations inspired many of his listeners.

> ... Gladstone like thunder sends
> His voice abroad - to earth's remotest ends
> The sound might well go forth - the awful works
> Constantly perpetrated by the Turks
> Call loudly for a strong avenging hand.
> Let us defend that most afflicted land.[3]

Gladstone's success at the election convinced him that a 'single issue' was the answer to party unity. However, his next choice, that of Home Rule for Ireland, announced in 1886, had profound consequences for the Liberal Party. Contrary to Gladstone's hopes, it provoked irreconcilable differences within the party. Moderate Liberals, led by Lord Hartington, viewed Home Rule as undermining both the English constitution and the British Empire. They deserted the Liberal Party and were subsequently known as Liberal Imperialists. Home Rule was Gladstone's political swan song. He clung to his aspirations that he could defeat the dogmatic opposition of the House of Lords. His fail-ures left the Liberal Party bereft of clear political ideas.

ii) Joseph Chamberlain and the Radical Alternative

One of the main challengers to Gladstone's policies was Joseph Chamberlain. He had entered Parliament in 1876 with a well-estab-lished Radical reputation, having been mayor of Birmingham, but his energetic pursuit of radical policies at a national level made him enemies. In particular, Chamberlain argued for a more collective demonstration of the people's will. There must be active democratic participation by the people so that policies could be designed to meet their needs. At Warrington, in September 1885, he upheld the demo-cratic rights of the people.

> Two millions of voices hitherto silent or unheard will now demand attention, and the claims that they may make, the wants that they express, and the rights upon which they insist, will be potent factors in our future legislation.[4]

The same year, Chamberlain published his Radical Programme, enti-tled the 'Unauthorised Programme' because it was not supported by the government. Although subsequent Liberal Governments adopted the very reforms Chamberlain advocated - land reform, payment of MPs, reform of the House of Lords and manhood suffrage - Chamberlain's radicalism was too polemical for moderate Liberals. Then Chamberlain resigned from the party in protest over Home Rule, so terminating his career as a Radical Liberal. It was left to other radical thinkers to redefine future Liberal thought.

iii) The Liberal Imperialists

The Liberal Imperialists were the third group to re-evaluate Liberal political philosophy. Led by Lord Rosebery, successor to Gladstone in 1894, they feared that greater democracy would encourage socialism and class conflict. Thus they propounded a policy of imperialism, arguing that this would unite all classes and avert the socialist threat.

Three beneficial effects would ensue from imperialism. Firstly, imperialism would be a civilising force, encouraging self-improve-ment amongst those fortunate enough to be brought under British rule. Secondly, trade within the Empire would flourish, generating sufficient income to fund domestic reforms. Finally, imperialism would be a unifying force, overcoming the inherent dangers of sectionalism. It would enhance the perception of the Liberal Party as a national party, appealing to all sections of the electorate. However, the language and ideas of Liberal Imperialism would be less strident, less jingoistic than that of the Conservative Party.

Was this the policy to revitalise the Liberal Party? For Rosebery and his fellow imperialists, Asquith, Lord Grey and Lord Haldane, the testing time proved to be the Boer War of 1899-1902. Popular opinion swung enthusiastically behind imperialists in both political parties. But as the harsh realities of the war filtered home - the use of Chinese slaves, the reality of Kitchener's concentration camps - imperialism was discredited. Like the Conservative Government, the Liberal Imperialists discovered that the electorate's support for imperialism was short-lived. Although imperialism had captured people's imaginations, it did not bring the promised economic benefits. The working classes in particular felt that they had little to gain from its continuation.

iv) New Liberalism

With the Liberal Imperialists unable to offer a convincing political creed for the new electorate, it was left to another group of thinkers to challenge and redefine Liberal party policy. However, they rejected the individualism of nineteenth-century Gladstonian Liberalism because they regarded the principles of *laissez-faire* as outdated.

New ideas were advanced which focused on the concept that society had to be viewed as a single, interlocking unit. Franchise reform had empowered a wide spectrum of citizens. Each had a responsibility to each other; each group of citizens was now interdependent. Therefore, everyone within society had common interests which could only be protected by the whole society. Only the State could exercise that responsibility, acting collectively on behalf of everyone. With democratic control of the State, the interests of the majority, not a minority, would be preserved. This political philosophy, which contrasted sharply with *laissez-faire* politics, was known as collectivism.

Two significant writers responsible for establishing this intellectual thought, known as New Liberalism, were the sociologist J.T. Hobhouse and the economist J.A. Hobson. Both attacked the ideas of imperialism because it upheld the interests of a minority over those of a majority. Both proclaimed the merits of a more democratic state. In his book, *Imperialism: A Study* (1902), Hobson criticised imperialism extensively because it threatened peace, encouraged national aggrandisement and concentrated national resources on military expenditure. Its greatest impact was that it diverted attention away from domestic problems. In particular, those who benefited from an aggressive foreign policy saw no purpose in ending the exploitation.

1 The vested interests, which, ... are shown to be chief promoters of an imperialist policy, play for a double stake, seeking their private commercial and financial gains at the expense and peril of the commonwealth. They at the same time protect their economic and political supremacy
5 at home against movements of popular reform. The city ground landlord, the country squire, the banker, the usurer, and the financier, ... the great

export manufacturers and merchants, the clergy of the State Church, the universities and great public schools, … have, both in Great Britain and on the Continent, drawn together for common political resistance
10 against attacks upon the power, the property, and the privileges which in various forms and degrees they represent. Having conceded under pressure the form of political power in the shape of elective institutions and a wide franchise to the masses, they are struggling to prevent the masses from gaining the substance of this power and using it for the establish-
15 ment of equality of economic opportunities.[5]

Hobhouse, likewise, in his book, *Democracy and Reaction* (1904), launched a twofold attack on imperialism. Whereas liberalism fostered self-government, imperialism promoted racial superiority. In this respect democracy and imperialism were totally incompatible because one advocated 'autonomy', the other 'ascendancy'. In addition, the preoccupation with imperialism had halted any hope of further domestic reform.

1 Both the friends and enemies of democracy inclined to the belief that when the people came into power there would be a time of rapid and radical domestic change combined in all probability with peace abroad ….As it turned out, almost the first act of the new British democracy
5 was to install the Conservatives in power, and to maintain them with but partial exceptions for nearly twenty years. Never were the fears or hopes of either side more signally disappointed. Before the event the advocates of popular government believed that they had now forged the necessary weapon of social advancement. There would be a new epoch
10 of internal reform. Political democracy was in substance achieved, and the time was ripe for a series of social reforms which … would amount to an even greater revolution. … The question how to reorganise society as a democratic State, not for a military but for an industrial life, not in the two great classes of exploiters and exploited but in an undi-
15 vided community, how to equalise opportunity, minimise the causes of poverty, choke up the sources of crime … such were the questions in which the best minds were absorbed, and which they believed would occupy the coming generation.[6]

How exactly did Hobson and Hobhouse plan to 'equalise opportunity'? The solution was to enhance the role of the State. The State had a collective responsibility to deploy its resources so as to minimise economic inequality. Only the State had the power to arbitrate in favour of the disadvantaged. Such redistribution of wealth was justified because everyone was part of the same community, with interdependent interests. Hobson argued, for example, that if the unearned wealth of the rich was taxed, this could be redistributed to increase the consumption power of the working classes.

The philosophies of Hobson and Hobhouse laid important foundations for twentieth-century liberalism. By viewing society as a whole, they hoped to avoid the dangerous doctrines of class politics. Labour could be retained as a significant ally because workers would identify with Liberal reforms. Rosebery's successor, Campbell-Bannerman, perceived the importance of advancing constructive policies which would transcend class differences. Thus those recently enfranchised would welcome the tenets of liberalism because, as Campbell-Bannerman envisaged, liberalism represented a 'broad church' in which they were valued members.

However, as well as forging this relationship with Labour, liberalism would not forsake its traditional principles. By 1905, the Conservative Government was damaged by the effects of tariff reform (the imposition of taxes on imports from outside the Empire), an unpopular Education Act, and a discredited foreign policy. Seizing their chance, the Liberals resurrected their advocacy of free trade. Their victory in the 1905 general election gave them the opportunity at last to implement some of their ideas.

b) The Conservative Party

The Conservatives faced an interesting dilemma in 1867. They were the architects of radical reform, but did they really endorse the principle of greater democracy? Disraeli had successfully defeated Gladstone only to find in 1868 that the new electorate was singularly unappreciative of the Conservatives' achievements, preferring to elect Gladstone. How, therefore, should the Conservatives respond to this unexpected expansion in democratic representation? Unfortunately, the Conservatives had spent the last 20 years in opposition, unable to present a strong alternative to liberalism. Could Disraeli now revitalise Conservative policy and capture the imagination and aspirations of the voters?

i) Disraeli's Conservatism

One issue concerning Disraeli's conservatism was whether he genuinely intended to create a popular Conservative Party which would attract working-class support, or whether he was merely redefining the familiar themes of Toryism. In a key speech, given in Manchester in 1872, he attacked the radical forces of the Liberal Party which, he asserted, were destroying the traditional institutions of the country. However, the most notable quotation from the speech was the reference to '*Sanitas sanitatum, omnia sanitas*', meaning that health, above all else, should be a prime consideration of the government. Was this Disraeli's bid to appeal to the working class and create a more democratic conservatism?

In a second speech at Crystal Palace in London, 1872, Disraeli stated the following:

1   When I say 'Conservative',I use the word in its purest and loftiest sense.
    I mean that the people of England,and especially the working classes of
    England,are proud of belonging to a great country,and wish to maintain
    its greatness - that they are proud of belonging to an imperial country,
5   and are resolved to maintain,if they can,their empire - that they believe,
    on the whole,that the greatness and the empire of England are to be
    attributed to the ancient institutions of the land.[7]

What did Disraeli hope to achieve? Note his reference to 'a great
country', 'an imperial country', and 'ancient institutions'. These were
largely familiar tenets of conservatism. But this speech intentionally
addressed a wider audience. Imperialism was depicted as a unifying
factor, bringing all groups within society together. Thus the working
classes would be proud to contribute to the glory of the Empire.

Disraeli was an astute politician who foresaw that such policies
could also attract another group, the middle classes. The professional
middle classes and successful entrepreneurs were rapidly converting
to conservatism because they were alarmed by Liberal legislation and
radical policies on state intervention. Disraeli sought to harness
potential middle-class support by convincing them that they, too, were
essential to the success of the Empire.

Under Disraeli, Conservatism remained distinctly anti-democratic.
Disraeli had no intention of succumbing to egalitarianism. He hoped
that his policy would stifle rather than encourage any serious agitation
for further political change. By the time of his death in 1881,
Conservative policy was finely balanced between satisfying the needs of
the working class, encouraging their continual deference to the
leaders of a well-defined policy of imperialism and wooing the middle
classes.

ii) The Success and Failure of Imperialism, 1885-1900

Following Disraeli's death, the Conservative Party was first led by Lord
Salisbury in the Lords and Sir Stafford Northcote in the Commons.
But it was not until 1885 that Lord Salisbury emerged as the clear
leader, with the authority to direct Conservative policy. One of the
challengers to his leadership prior to 1885 had been the Conservative
MP Randolph Churchill. Churchill had urged the adoption of radical
social policies in order to make the Conservatives a party 'of the
people, for the people, by the people' (Blackpool, 24 January 1884).
But Churchill was vague as to how such ideas would be implemented.
As a result, the party rallied around Lord Salisbury and the policy
initiated by Disraeli, namely that of imperialism, formed the basis of
Conservative philosophy for the next 15 years.

Imperialism was a successful political philosophy. The
Conservatives exploited to full advantage the themes of monarchy,
the preservation of national institutions and the unity of the
kingdom. When Gladstone threatened that unity with Home Rule,

the Conservatives quickly advanced themselves as defenders of the realm. Home Rule was anathema to those who supported the Empire. If the links between Britain and Ireland were severed, it would encourage dissent amongst other colonies and so undermine the authority of the 'mother country'.

Like the Liberal Imperialists, the Conservatives envisaged that imperialism would constitute a viable alternative to the emerging policies of collectivism. Imperialism would gain working-class approval because of the prospect of cheaper goods from within the Empire. But by the end of the nineteenth century, these objectives were being undermined as the public reacted to revelations about the Boer War. Was imperialism justified when it diverted funds from domestic reform?

In 1903, Joseph Chamberlain launched a radical but ultimately disastrous proposal to gain the electorate's support. Chamberlain had joined the Conservatives as a Liberal Unionist in 1885 and was subsequently appointed colonial secretary. By 1903, he was certain that Britain should grant preferential treatment to imperial goods, posing higher tariffs on non-imperial goods. Thus Britain could avoid the pitfalls of economic depression by reducing her dependency on exports from outside the Empire. The income generated could then be directed towards social reform in Britain which would elicit working-class support. The fact that tariffs would also prove a desirable alternative to tax rises was considered an additional attraction. Despite his failure to obtain cabinet endorsement for these ideas, Chamberlain launched his policy of tariff reform in a famous speech in Birmingham on 15 May 1903.

It was a grave miscalculation. The Conservative Party, under Balfour's uncertain leadership, split between free traders and protectionists. The working classes doubted Chamberlain's argument that tariffs meant cheaper food. The Liberals exploited the economic worries of the working classes and convinced them that voting Conservative meant higher prices. The Liberals won the 1905 election.

Whereas during the last 20 years of the nineteenth century, imperialism appeared to have succesfully contained the aspirations of the new electorate, by 1900 the long-term effects of franchise reform were more apparent. The forces which were pressing for further domestic reforms were now too numerous to be ignored. It was the Liberals, not the Conservatives, who were best positioned to deliver those reforms.

3 Party Organisation

The second major impact of political reform was the need to restructure party organisations. As patronage declined, so voting behaviour became less predictable. The most obvious method of attracting votes and increasing support was to build up local associations which would encourage grass-root involvement in politics. Through these associations, the political education of the masses could be enacted. Over the next 30 years, both Conservatives and Liberals developed more sophisticated and efficient organisations. Both parties adopted similar methods each often learning from the experiences of the other. In the process, both succeeded in managing the transition to greater democracy.

i) Conservative Central Office
One distinguishing feature of the Conservative Party was that it remained a hierarchical party. In 1870, Disraeli created the Conservative Central Office, with John Gorst as its principal agent. The task of Central Office was to select candidates, manage party funds, act as the office for MPs in the Commons and publicise speeches of prominent Conservatives. But at no time could local party associations either challenge directives from Central Office or comment on policy, which remained the prerogative of the leadership. Indeed, the authority of Central Office was noticeably enhanced with the passing of the Corrupt Practices Act. Local patronage inevitably declined, enabling Central Office to play a more crucial role in the selection of candidates. In contrast to the Conservatives, however, the Liberals had no equivalent organisation.

ii) Political Associations
Both parties sought to mobilise grass-root support. The Conservatives responded first, founding the National Union of Conservative and Constitutional Associations in 1867. Its prime objective was to establish working men's clubs which acted essentially as propaganda organisations promoting conservatism. They maintained communications between Central Office and rank and file members, and provided the party with local activist support at elections. Membership was initially directed at the working classes because Disraeli foresaw that future electoral success depended on the urban vote. But under the leadership of Gorst, the network of clubs expanded to include associations which attracted the urban middle class. This was a crucial development. The Conservatives now had the appearance of embracing all sections of society rather than being socially exclusive. The rise in the Conservative urban vote was a major factor in the Conservative victory of 1874.

Unlike the Conservatives, the Liberals were slower to reorganise themselves in the aftermath of the 1867 Reform Act and in particular, they failed to nurture the new urban vote. Instead, they endeavoured to rectify their poor performance in rural areas. This was an uphill task, not least because they were unable to overcome long-term traditional support for the Conservatives. By 1874 the Conservatives had made great advances, whereas the Liberal Party seemed to be disintegrating, plagued by divisions, and totally disorganised.

Frustrated by the ignominy of defeat, the initiative for revival came from Joseph Chamberlain. Since 1865 Chamberlain had been a key member of the Birmingham Liberal Association, promoting more efficient party organisation and management of elections with the result that the Liberals won all three parliamentary seats in Birmingham in 1868. In 1877, he founded the National Liberal Federation (NLF). Chamberlain's vision of democracy was driven by a belief in direct participation of the people, and through the NLF he sought to implement democracy. Chamberlain created an organisational structure which ostensibly involved every citizen. Everyone, whether a voter or non-voter, could join their Liberal ward association (a ward being an area within a constituency). Here, Liberal politics would be discussed and views established on current policies. Delegates elected at ward meetings would attend an executive committee which, in a similar fashion, would appoint delegates to higher committees. Throughout this hierarchical structure, a two-way dialogue was established with opinions solicited, people consulted, and votes taken democratically. This contrasted sharply with the Conservative Party, where the rank and file could not exert any influence on policies.

The NLF was a powerful institution. It claimed to be more democratic than Parliament on the grounds that its authority did not emanate from a restricted franchise. Critics accused the NLF of being too arrogant and powerful. They considered that democracy was no longer based on consent but on authoritarian directives from the Birmingham Association controlled by Chamberlain. In fact the centralised control which Chamberlain seemed to be exerting was ultimately resisted by the local associations, who refused to act at his bidding. Their reiteration of support for Gladstone was seen as a victory for a more moderate interpretation of politics.

iii) Local Political Clubs

The local political club, whether Conservative or Liberal, was a successful institution. Each party appreciated the importance of making politics accessible to the man in the street. Often clubs were located in public houses, where social and political activity could be combined. Thus politics was made accessible to the working classes. As one observer commented:

> If possible avoid building & avoid elaborate furniture - the latter simply drives working men out of the place. Clean, bright, rooms, with the means of playing drafts & bagatelle is the chief want ... all our successes begin this way ...[8]

The middle classes also had their political clubs, such as the Leeds Liberal Club, the Manchester Reform Club, the Liverpool Conservative Club and the Scottish Conservative Club. These would frequently act as the local town's party headquarters. London likewise experienced an expansion in clubs although here the Conservative clubs outnumbered the Liberal ones. Nevertheless, whether at a national or local level, the political club functioned as a focal point for both political and social activity.

iv) The Primrose League and the Liberal League

In addition to the political clubs, both parties sought other means to encourage widespread support. Within the Conservative Party, the most successful institution was the Primrose League, founded by Randolph Churchill. The name, the Primrose League, emanated from the practice adopted by some Conservatives of remembering the anniversary of Disraeli's death, 19 April 1881, by placing a typical spring flower, the primrose, in their lapels. As an admirer of Disraeli, Churchill chose the name, Primrose League, as a way of sustaining the memory of Disraeli's leadership. Churchill appreciated the necessity of reaching out to the electorate, by making politics an accessible, integral part of their lives. Hundreds of local Primrose Leagues were founded throughout the country, providing the Conservative Party with loyal activists. The Primrose League acted as a propaganda agent for the Conservative Party, stoutly defending traditional Conservative principles. At elections, candidates could depend on their local Primrose League to rally the voters.

1   In every constituency in this country where there is a habitation of the Primrose League the Conservative candidate will have at his command a band of workers, a *corps d'élite*, volunteers and not mercenaries, representing and drawn from all classes of the community, united by
5   the most perfect equality, and pledged by honour and by the principles of their political faith to sacrifice their time ... to placing him at the head of the poll.[9]

The Liberals had several similar organisations. The Liberal League, for example, founded in 1886, closely resembled the Primrose League. In its publication, *The Liberal and Radical*, the Liberal League defined itself as a

> democratic association formed to combine men and women in the promotion of Liberal principles. ... the Liberal League has determined to go out into the streets and parks, and, meeting the democracy, there attempt to politically educate the masses.[10]

Through these associations, politics came to the people, subtly disguised in the form of popular entertainment: tea dances, excursions, summer fetes, cricket matches and garden parties. Political education would be a feature of the entertainment, but was never permitted to detract from social enjoyment. One of the Primrose League's most successful achievements was its mobilisation of female party workers. By demonstrating their efficiency and excellent organisational skills within the League, many of these women unwittingly supported the suffragette argument that women were effective in politics. For the Liberals, the combination of light entertainment and the dissemination of political ideas was an ideal method of political education. It clearly helped to delay the defection of the working classes to socialism.

v) The Role of the Press

For both political parties, broad press coverage was essential to the dissemination of political ideas. Although local political associations could publish their own pamphlets and advertise local meetings, their readership was limited. The expansion of the provincial press after 1867 was, therefore, a significant factor in popularising politics. Circulation figures of local papers such as the *Yorkshire Post* and the *Leeds Mercury* increased as people sought up-to-date news.

Newspapers had their own political affiliations. The *Manchester Guardian* was a prominent Liberal newspaper whilst *The Scotsman* showed a Conservative bias. Yet, in his analysis of the expansion of the provincial press, J.A. Hamer argued that the Liberals gained a distinct advantage because of 'the overwhelming numerical supriority of the Liberal press' which, as the Conservatives realised, enabled Liberals to reach the working classes.[11]

In addition to the respectable provincial newspapers, the appetite for news was met by the growth of cheaper publications such as news-sheets. Critics attacked them because they only contained fragments of news, punctured with sensationalised headlines which the man in the street could quickly digest, before turning to read about his latest passions, cricket and football. It could be argued that these were the precursors of the tabloid press today, where strong opinions grab the headlines, but lack in-depth news anaylsis. M. Ostrogorski commented:

1   … with the development of the cheap Press, a workman can buy a newspaper all to himself for a halfpenny, and can read it alone and take what he likes from it. Being full of small items of news, the paper, instead of concentrating the attention of the reader, makes it flit from paragraph
5   to paragraph, and in the long run brings more weariness than rest or food to the mind. As a rule, there is only one part which is read with serious attention, - the columns devoted to sport. The interest in sport, including betting, has become a regular endemic disease, which ravages the country.[12]

Hobhouse queried whether democracy could really function if opinion was corrupted and moral standards lowered because of prejudice generated by the cheap press. Hobhouse's views actually reflected a very serious concern. Despite the beneficial effects of education (see pages 75-81), growing literacy, the expansion of the press, and the growth of party organisations, a substantial section of the population still remained indifferent to politics.

4 Conclusion

The intellectual climate which had prevailed until 1867 underwent significant changes thereafter as politicians adjusted to the needs of a wider democracy. Britain was still a limited parliamentary democracy, but now the operation of government had to change. In particular, it was clear that power was increasingly invested in the people and that government had to be accountable to them.

The electoral reforms of 1872-85 rendered this accountability essential. Despite the fact that many politicians were still contemptuous of the masses, they now ignored them at their peril. Although neither party managed the transition to greater democracy very smoothly, each appreciated the necessity to devise rational policies which could win votes. Parties sought to elicit voters' support by issuing party manifestos outlining their particular political ideas. Likewise, the successful delivery of such ideas depended on efficient party organisation. Alongside the proliferation of political associations there were also important developments in the management of elections. By the late 1880s both parties had abandoned their dependency on part-time, often corrupt volunteers and had appointed full-time, paid election managers and party agents, a development clearly attributable to the effects of the Corrupt Practices Act. These agents organised mass meetings at which candidates would deliver rousing oratories on key issues. Likewise the regular updating of electoral registers became common practice. Thus, aided by a nationwide network of clubs and associations, together with rapid circulation of news and more sophisticated management of elections, political parties were able to educate the masses. In addition, political parties were better informed about the opinions of the people.

What were the long-term consequences of wider political involvement? First, the extension of the franchise to a majority of the male electorate was progress, but it still left 40 per cent of all adult males plus all women disenfranchised. How long would it be before further reform was demanded? Secondly, both parties sought to retain their traditional supporters and to win new converts, hoping that their political views would deflect any interest in the dangers of socialism. As will be discussed in the ensuing chapter, however, neither the disenfranchised working class nor women were prepared to tolerate the *status quo* for much longer.

References

1   William Ansell Day, *The Conservative Party and the County Franchise*, 2nd edn, (Wyman and Sons, 1883), pp.4-5.
2   Havelock Fisher, *The Assimulation of County and Borough Franchise* (Simpkin, Marshall & Co, 1883), pp.7-8.
3   R. Newcombe, *A Poetical Life of the Right Hon. W.E. Gladstone, M.P.* (London, 10, Paternoster Row, 1880), p.15.
4   Joseph Chamberlain, 'The Radical Platform', in *Speeches by the Right Hon. Joseph Chamberlain, M.P* (Simpkin, Marshall & Co, 1885), p.14.
5   J.A. Hobson, *Imperialism: A Study* (James Nisbett & Co. Ltd, 1902), p.150.
6   L.T. Hobhouse, *Democracy and Reaction* (T. Fisher Unwin, 1904), pp.49-52.
7   Benjamin Disraeli, 24 June 1872, cited in Brian Macarthur (ed), *The Penguin Book of Historic Speeches* (Penguin, 1996), p.320.

8   Cited in H.J. Hanham, *Elections and Party Management in the Time of Disraeli and Gladstone* (The Harvester Press, 1978), p.104.

9   H.W. Lucy (ed), *Speeches of Lord Randolph Churchill* (Routledge & Sons, 1885), p.120.

10 *Liberal and Radical*, 3 September 1887, p.172.

11 Hanham, *Elections and Party Management*, p.112.

12 M. Ostrogorski, *Democracy and the Organization of Political Parties*, vol.1(MacMillan & Co. Ltd, 1902) pp.401-2.

Source-based questions on 'The Growth of Party Politics, 1868-1906'

1. *Two opinions on the extension of the franchise*

Read the extracts by William Ansell Day and Havelock Fisher on page 58. Answer the following questions.

a) Explain what Day means by 'exploded dogma' in line 5. (3 marks)

b) What was Day's main argument against extending the franchise? What may have been his motive for this argument? (4 marks)

c) In what ways does Havelock Fisher disagree with Day on the need to grant County householders the vote? (4 marks)

d) To what extent do Day and Fisher share the same views despite their different political backgrounds? Explain your answer. (6 marks)

e) With reference to both extracts, evaluate the extent to which there was continuity and change in attitudes between 1867 and 1884 towards democratic reform. (8 marks)

2. *'The Crisis of Liberalism'*

Read the two extracts from Hobson and Hobhouse on pages 62-63 and answer the following questions.

a) Give two examples of what Hobson meant by 'vested interests' (line 1). (2 marks)

b) What, in Hobhouse's opinion, was the link between democracy and social advancement? (3 marks)

c) Hobhouse refers to 'an undivided community' (lines 14-15). Using your own knowledge, plus the extract, explain how this vision of liberalism differed from the traditional principles of liberalism? (6 marks)

d) To what extent does Hobson agree or disagree with Hobhouse that political democracy had been of limited success? Explain your answer. (6 marks)

e) To what extent are these accounts reliable evidence of the problems facing the Liberal Party at the end of the nineteenth century? (8 marks)

Hints and advice: Your first task is to read these four documents carefully and to check your understanding of each one. You should identify key words and phrases which help to explain the overall meaning of the document. For example, the phrase 'if the franchise were a right and not a privilege' (lines 3-4) could be the clue to appreciating William Ansell Day's central argument. Analysing the language and style of the document is essential because it also gives you insights into the author's attitude. Does the author adopt a critical or a complimentary tone? Do his words indicate a particular bias?

Question 2a is a typical, short answer question. A brief, relevant response is required, demonstrating that you have understood the words 'vested interests'. If you are unsure, see if you can establish from the rest of the text what Hobson means. 'Interests' should be straightforward, but you will only get full marks if you can define 'vested' as well. Do the words 'private' and 'gains' (lines 2-3) provide any further insights?

Question 2b tests your appreciation of the two main thrusts of Hobhouse's arguments. Be careful not to make a simple comment that democracy was necessary before social reform could occur. You should try to formulate a brief analysis of why granting power to the people would result in domestic reform. Point out what conditions were now present which had previously been absent.

Document questions like 2c frequently require deployment of external knowledge. Use this opportunity to demonstrate your overall understanding of liberalism as well as the manner in which this political philosophy was being re-assessed. Show that you have grasped key words deployed in the book: *laissez-faire*, individualism, as well as collectivism. Focus on the fact that you have to identify differences. Each sentence in your answer should analyse at least one comparison between the two visions of liberalism.

Question 2d requires you to cross-reference the two documents. There are a number of similar comments in each, but do not assume that the documents will either totally agree or disagree with each other. You should always avoid describing what one author says first, then the other. Identify points of similarity such as 'vested interests' and 'enemies of democracy' and explain what each author intended with those comments. How does each of them express their disappointment that the successes of popular reform were subsequently thwarted?

Questions like 2e often challenge your ability not only to deploy extensive knowledge but also to test the reliability of the source. For 2e you would have to explain what the two documents perceive to be the nature of the problems facing the Liberal Party. You would then need to evaluate the reliability of the two authors. Does their background explain the views they present? What was the motive of each author when writing his book? Does your own knowledge support their statements or is there relevant evidence which gives an alternative explanation for Liberal problems?

Summary Diagram
The Growth of Party Politics, 1868-1906

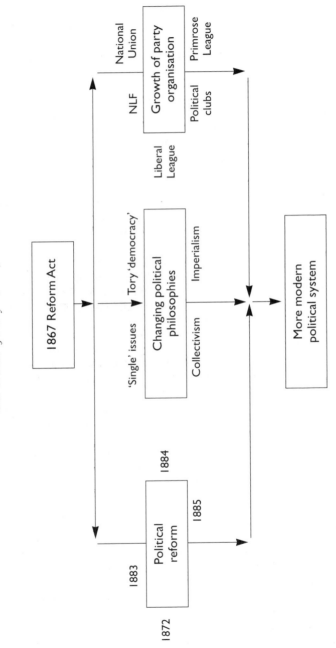

5 Education, Labour and Women, 1868-1906

Although the Reform Acts of 1867 and 1884-5 had extended the franchise, Britain was far from being a democratic country. There was still not 'one man, one vote' - let alone 'one person, one vote'. The franchise was limited to men and, furthermore, only to those men who owned or occupied property. Most members of the upper and middle classes, as in earlier decades, believed that only they themselves could produce good government, and they dismissed the working classes as incapable of making much of a contribution. Yet after 1884 working-class voters were in a majority in many constituencies, and hence their potential power was enormous. They might be able not only to challenge the political power of the traditional governing classes but also, perhaps, to undermine their social superiority. As a result, many politicians were determined to nurture these voters into an acceptance of the existing hierarchical society so that, despite possessing the vote, they should continue to show deference to their 'superiors'. In this way, they hoped to check what they saw as the dangers of democracy.

One method by which governments planned to control the threat of democracy was through education. It was important to strike a balance between having a skilled and literate working class for the sake of promoting the economy, and limiting the scope of educational provision so that people did not seek to question social or political injustices. In one respect, this policy of social conditioning was successful. British workers never pursued the path of revolution. Yet, in other respects, it failed. One of the implications of a more universal system of education was that different groups of people acquired new aspirations and expectations. The working classes began to appreciate that Parliament did not always best serve their interests. Likewise, women became more conscious of their political inequality. The challenges of class and gender were crucial in helping to shape the emerging democratic state. Without changes in education, these challenges would have been slower to materialise.

1 Education and Democracy

There were two interrelated issues within education which were to determine attitudes towards the emergence of greater political democracy. First, politicians felt that they ought to be involved in both state and private education in order to 'manage' its effects: their clear intention was to use education as a form of indoctrination whereby the working classes would be conditioned to accept the *status quo*. The second issue concerned working-class initiatives. These served partially to counteract the state 'restrictions'. As the working class widened their educational opportunities through their own enterprises, so they gained the very confidence which the government had tried to suppress. The result of this newly acquired confidence was the realisation that there could be some merit in pursuing a more independent political agenda. The fact that a working-class political party, the Independent Labour Party, was founded in 1893 was due at least in part to the impact of a more universal system of education.

a) The Role of the State

i) Private Education

Politicians considered the development of education for the masses as a vital policy to be implemented in parallel with political progress. In 1867, the government had trusted approximately one million urban workers with the vote, but it was important that they exercise this privilege prudently. There had to be continued respect for the nation's institutions. Moreover, the principles of representation, namely that the vote was still a privilege not a right, must not be undermined. What role could the state play, therefore, in encouraging men to exercise their new responsibilities sensibly?

One approach was to maintain and promote a hierarchical society. Whatever education the workers received, that of their 'superiors' had to be better, fitting them for their role as leaders. Not surprisingly, this reinforced upper- and middle-class contempt for ordinary people and the idea that they should exercise any effective responsibility in the democratic process.

The growth of the 'public schools' and grammar schools was a key factor in creating a hierarchical education system. Public schools were expensive boarding schools, such as Eton, Winchester and Harrow, which catered for the sons of the landowning nobility and gentry. Reforming headmasters such Thomas Arnold (Rugby School, 1828-42) and Edward Thring (Uppingham School, 1853-87) were instrumental in establishing the character and ethos of public school education in the second half of the century. Not only did they widen the curriculum beyond that of the standard classical education to include science, modern languages, games and music, they also emphasised the importance of training boys for their roles as governors and defenders of the Empire.

This elitist objective encouraged a corresponding shift in aims amongst the grammar schools. These had originally educated sons of the middle classes as well as poorer boys whose fees were paid for by charitable foundations. Yet under the Endowed Schools Act of 1869 (see page 78), good, cheap education became the privilege of the middle classes, who offered little objection to the exclusion of the lower orders. Likewise, they endorsed the decisions by schools such as Harrow, Repton and Rugby to establish separate local schools to cater for those of lower status, such as sons of tradesmen and farmers. Many schools changed from being a local grammar school to a fee paying, public boarding school and so contributed to the increasingly exclusive nature of the English education system.

Public school education was a crucial component of a policy designed to mould the character and attitudes of the ruling class in Britain. From the classrooms of the public schools emerged the elite whose purpose was to promote the interests of Britain and its Empire. They were educated to be tough, honest and good fighting men, but scant attention was paid to their intellectual education. Thus the future leaders of the country were trained on the playing fields of England's public schools.

ii) State Education

As Robert Lowe argued in 1867, democracy was endangered if controlled by the uneducated. The challenge for governments after 1867 was how to give due recognition to the new political status of the working class without encouraging their disrespect for a hierarchical society. Part of the answer rested in the educational policies adopted between 1870 and 1902 (see page 78). Forster's Education Act of 1870 was the first major piece of legislation to tackle the issue of working class education.

In his speech to the House of Commons on 17 February 1870, W.E. Forster said:

1   Upon the speedy provision of elementary education depends our industrial prosperity. It is no use trying to give technical teaching to our artisans without elementary education; uneducated labourers ... are for the most part, unskilled labourers, and if we leave our work-folk any
5   longer unskilled, ... they will become over-matched in the competition of the world. Upon this speedy provision depends also, I fully believe, the good, the safe working of our constitutional system. To its honour, Parliament has lately decided that England shall in future be governed by popular government. I am one of those who would not wait until the
10 people were educated before I would trust them with political power. If we had thus waited we might have waited long for education; but now that we have given them political power we must not wait any longer to give them education. ...[1]

Forster's comments were revealing on two accounts. He acknowledged the disparity which prevailed between the political power of the working classes, which was growing, and the potential of their economic worth, which would only be evident once they were properly educated. Hence Britain's dominance as an industrial power would be jeopardised unless the workforce was capable of responding to foreign economic challenges.

There was, however, another danger: that to the 'safe working of our constitutional system'. The smooth operation of parliamentary government would be weakened by the impact of an inexperienced

Educational legislation - key developments

1869 Endowed Schools Act

Until 1869, grammar schools were funded by endowments which enabled local poor children to attend. This act permitted endowed funds to be used for other purposes. As a result, local children were increasingly denied access to grammar schools and the chance of cheap secondary education. Thus the grammar schools ceased to be local schools.

1870 Forster's Education Act

This laid the foundations for the elementary education of the working classes. Essential points were:

1) The establishment of School Boards in areas where there were no voluntary schools i.e. schools funded by the Anglican Church. These Boards would set up elementary schools funded by ratepayers.

2) The Cowper-Temple amendment to the 1870 bill ensured that there would be no religious teaching in Board Schools.

3) Denominational schools would receive grants paid for out of taxes not local rates.

1876 Education Act

This Act was designed to support the voluntary schools by encouraging attendance especially in rural areas. The Tories, under Disraeli, were concerned to discourage the spread of the undenominational Board Schools.

1880 Education Act

Compulsory elementary school attendance was introduced.

1891 Elementary Education Act

Schools could admit children aged between 3 and 15 free of charge and claim a state grant as payment.

1899 Board of Education created

Established one central authority for elementary and secondary education.

1902 Education Act

School Boards were abolished. Newly created Local Education Authorities under the County and County Borough Councils now administered elementary and secondary education. The Act instituted statutory secondary education.

and poorly educated electorate because ignorance was dangerous. In this respect, education for the masses had to ensure that the political survival of the natural elite, the upper and middle classes, was not undermined. Thus the state would instil the working class with attitudes of deference and passive acceptance of what their 'betters' decided. Hence whilst universal elementary education was implemented, nothing was done to challenge the methodology of teaching, which stultified the minds of young children. Rote learning continued to be the dominant teaching method, its effect being to discourage active learning. Initiative was stifled.

Successive governments' concerns to match political progress with educational progress were exemplified first by the introduction of compulsory and then by free, elementary education (see page 78). In 1884 and 1885, scientific and technical education was expanded with institutions such as the City and Guilds of London acting as pioneers in this field. Yet in 1895 the very fears articulated by Forster in 1870 were reiterated by the Bryce Commission on Secondary Education. The Commission referred to the real disadvantages 'from which young Englishmen suffer in industry and commerce owing to the superior preparation of their competitors in several countries of continental Europe'.[2] It would seem that Forster's determination to meet the economic challenge of a fast developing world had not been entirely successful. This awareness of the deficiencies in education led to the 1902 Education Act.

In introducing his Education Bill, A.J. Balfour admitted that, despite advances,

> these University colleges and these great technological institutions do not, cannot, and never will effect all they might do so long as our secondary education, which is their necessary preparation, is in the imperfect condition in which we find it.[3]

The 1902 Act was a landmark in terms of establishing compulsory secondary education. However, the method by which this system was to be implemented ensured that both the Church and the upper and middle classes retained control of education. The abolition of the Board schools and the fact that denominational schools were now funded by local rates, as opposed to national taxes, proved controversial. This decision reversed the principles established in 1870 (see page 78). Nonconformists were outraged that, once again, they would have to fund Church schools directly through their local taxes. Moreover, education was now controlled by county and county borough councils, which were mainly dominated by the upper and middle classes.

By 1906, the effects of government education policies were clear. The nature of educational provision ensured that deference and respect for the ruling classes continued. Traditional values were inculcated, resulting in an acceptance by the working classes of their limited role in the emerging democratic state. Consequently, no working class political party challenged the upper and middle classes' monopoly on government until the twentieth century. The dominance of the Conservative Party in government between 1885 and 1906 was further proof that they had successfully checked the dangers of socialism (see page 80). Thus the implementation of social conditioning would appear, at face value, to have worked. Yet were there not some inherent dangers in this hidden agenda of subservience? Was Britain's subsequent decline as a world power not due, at least in part, to the failure of her governments to appreciate in time the merits of full democracy?

b) Working-Class Initiatives

If governments assumed that they could mould the character of the working class through their manipulation of education then they were mistaken. One of the consequences of their policies was that incentives to improve educationally came not only from above but also from below. Several key factors prompted this development. Firstly, many members of the working class began to realise that it was only through an understanding of economics and politics that they could seek to change their own conditions. Their goals were essentially materialistic, with improved working conditions, hours of work and wages being their priority. These objectives could not be achieved if people were inarticulate and ignorant of either economics or politics. Therefore, following the middle-class example of self-help, independent working-class educational initiatives developed.

Secondly, working-class interest in education was stimulated by the impact of a severe depression in the 1880s which encouraged more militant activity. New working-class leaders emerged, many deriving their politics from backgrounds of great hardship. Their political objectives were channelled through the 'new unionism', unions which represented the unskilled worker (see page 83), and through socialist organisations. In addition, socialist leaders like Tom Mann, Keir Hardie and Will Thorne, leader of the Gasworkers' Union, all set personal examples of pursuing self-education as a means of improving themselves.

Thirdly, the involvement of socialists in encouraging working-class education was crucial. Their ulterior purpose was clear. People had to be educated in the ideas of socialism so that, with appropriate training, they would adopt socialism as a political ideal. Socialism was the doctrine that society should be based not on conflict and inequality, as occurred under capitalism, but on equality. This would be achieved by promoting the collective welfare of all workers and above all, through the common ownership of the means of production. The Social Democratic Federation (SDF), founded by H.M. Hyndman in 1881, aimed to 'educate', 'agitate' and 'organise'[4] in order to spread the ideals of socialism. William Morris's Socialist League likewise regarded education as an essential prerequisite for the political emancipation of the working classes. Children were also a vital target through whom political and economic awareness could be raised. The Socialist Sunday School movement, with its emphasis on secular, socialist teachings, involved around 5,000 children at its peak in the mid-1890s. Socialists were acutely aware of the potential political power the young would eventually wield, given the extension of the franchise.

A successful working-class press also propounded socialist views with papers like the *Labour Prophet* and the *Labour Leader*, as well as the *Clarion*, which had a weekly readership of 80,000. A proliferation of cheap broadsheets, periodicals and pamphlets helped to spread socialist ideals throughout the country. Lectures and classes supplemented the spread of knowledge. In Northumberland and Durham, lectures in political economy, elementary science and history provided by the University Extension movement attracted an attendance of over 1,000 miners. Their enthusiasm only dampened when strikes in 1887 deprived them of the means for paying for classes.

c) Conclusion

What impact did education have on attitudes towards democracy by the end of the nineteenth century? In one respect, governments had sought to use education as a means of 'managing' (i.e. minimising) democracy. They had only to glance across the Channel to Europe to witness the dangers which occurred if revolutionary ideas gained a foothold in society. The idea that the British working class would ever wield political power did not, to them, bear contemplation. Although governments perceived the need for a more articulate and intelligent working class, its role had to be limited to assisting the middle classes in becoming the ruling group. Yet this was a potentially dangerous strategy to pursue. Education could turn out to be a Pandora's Box.

Viewed from a different perspective, greater educational opportunities alerted the working classes to the fact that there were political, social and economic injustices in society. Although they remained largely respectful of the country's traditional institutions, the working classes now sought greater political involvement for which independent working-class educational initiatives were an essential development. A natural corollary, however, to greater political awareness was the realisation that the established democratic model was deficient. The extension of the franchise had not necessarily benefited working-class interests. It was then imperative to create independent labour representation in order to challenge and reform these injustices.

2 Class and Democracy

Following the Reform Acts of 1867 and 1884, the working classes constituted the majority of the voting population in both urban and rural areas. Did their newly acquired political influence result in a desire for greater popular representation in Parliament or even an independent political party? If so, why did the British working-class party develop within a peaceful, constitutional framework rather than as the result of a class struggle? What is clear is that the impetus to establish an independent working man's political party progressed slowly, with the majority in the working class content to vote for the existing parties. But why was there no working-class political party until the end of the nineteenth century? This requires explanation because it is fundamental to understanding the evolutionary nature of British democracy.

a) The Trade Union Movement

The trade union movement epitomised the conservative nature of the working class. The political and economic grievances which had characterised the Chartist movement had largely been addressed and no longer seemed so significant. Subsequent governments had established a relationship of mutual respect with the trade unions, assisted by a steady legislative programme of trade union and factory reforms. The unions, themselves, represented the skilled and relatively well-off members of the working class. The orthodox economics of liberalism, as exemplified by free trade and individualism, had brought them benefits which they were loath to lose. Yet neither political party was able to retain the consistent allegiance of trade unions. Gladstone's Irish policies cost him valuable popular support in 1886, whilst the Tories' policy of tariff reform, announced in 1903, frightened the working classes into voting solidly for the Liberal policy of free trade.

Throughout the last decades of the century, the trade union movement had limited political goals. Its priority was to seek the election of working men who would represent their interests sympathetically in Parliament. An acceptance of the principles of nineteenth-century liberal parliamentary government pervaded trade union politics. Hence, the first working-class MPs, Alexander Macdonald and Thomas Burt, two miners elected in 1874, were both Liberals. By 1890, there were only eight working-class MPs. It was important, at this stage, for the Trade Union Congress to maintain cooperation with the main political parties. The movement as a whole lacked cohesion and so was too weak to act independently in politics. Thus the aims of the TUC were distinctly cautious and moderate, as well as acceptable to both Liberal and Conservative parties. In addition, its vehemently anti-socialist stance deterred attempts to achieve more working-class political involvement.

By 1900 there were some who argued that the trade unions should play a more positive role in shaping the form of the democratic state. These included the Fabians, Sidney and Beatrice Webb. Founded in 1884, the Fabian Society consisted of middle-class intellectuals whose socialism provided a distinctive alternative to Marx's philosophy of class conflict. They advocated the gradual 'permeation' of socialism up through local politics to the national level where all the parties would be affected. Intelligent and educated socialists had to lead the masses, using their superior expertise and knowledge in order to secure the best interests of the working class. Trade unionists were particularly important because they were able to deploy their knowledge and skills on behalf of their members whilst also being the natural candidates to provide professional working-class representation in parliament. In the opinion of the Webbs, trade union involvement was fundamental to the delivery of working-class political education and to the future development of working-class democracy by peaceful, constitutional means.

The other significant influence on trade union thought was the emergence of New Unionism. The New Unions were distinct from the more traditional trade unions in that they recruited not from the skilled sector but from the much more numerous unskilled sectors - including the dockers, the gasworkers and the seamen. The main trade union movement had accepted the 'dominant ideology' of orthodox economics, as can be seen in their banners. Their tactics were nonconfrontational and their politics distinctly apolitical. The proponents of New Unionism, however, envisaged a more direct and confrontational approach. They constituted an organised, ideological movement which sought to politicise the workers. Hit by the deepening depression of the 1880s, unskilled workers were attracted by the fighting language of New Unionism, which talked of the right to a 'living wage', to be realised, if necessary, through strike action. In the new collectivist state, every worker would attain equality. With no previous political associations, such as that of more traditional trade unionists with the Liberal Party, New Unionists exploited the economic grievances of unskilled workers to encourage industrial confrontation and even class warfare.

What were the implications of New Unionism for the development of democracy? Unfortunately for those who were dedicated socialists the movement rapidly lost momentum. Although there had been progress with the unionisation of new groups of workers, there were also setbacks, especially as employers retaliated successfully against union militancy in the 1890s. What New Unionism did achieve was effectively to strengthen the non-socialist camp. Its failure to win large numbers of converts provides an excellent illustration of why the British working class did not follow a more revolutionary path. Its inability to win the minds of the labour movement helps to explain the aversion to doctrinal politics which was to be the hallmark of the new independent working class political movement.

One perceptive insight into the nature of British socialism at the end of the century comes from the historian E.H. Hunt. In his comprehensive analysis of British labour history, Hunt sought to break away from doctrinal viewpoints and evaluate the development of the British labour movement within a wider context of social history, demography and the role of domestic labour. He commented, 'From the mid 1890s onwards what was usually understood by "socialism" in Britain was a constitutional reformism that was opportunist, pragmatic, lacking in ideological perspective, and not easily distinguished from advanced Liberalism'.[5]

b) Working-Class Attitudes

It is not sufficient, however, merely to evaluate the role of trade unions in determining the future shape of democracy in Britain. If trade unions were the conservative strand within the British labour movement, were there additional influences which contributed to the emergence of an independent working-class political movement by the end of the century?

It is important to appreciate that in 1901 only 15 per cent of the total employed workforce were trade unionists. What characterised the attitudes of the remaining 85 per cent towards democracy and why were they apparently slow to progress towards independent working-class representation? How can the conservative nature of the British working class be explained?

It is the Marxist view, as expounded by historians such as Eric Hobsbawm, that a labour aristocracy, a working-class elite, had emerged whose affluence contrasted with that of the rest of the labour movement. This group exercised a distinctive influence in that they argued against militancy and discouraged the concept of class struggle. Had this affluent section not existed, there would have been greater consensus on the need for a class struggle, a view which would fit in neatly with Marxist theory.

Another view is propounded by Ross McKibbin who, in his investigation into the reasons for the failure of Marxism in Britain, portrays a working class which was fragmented and diversified. Local interests prevailed at the expense of a common working-class ideology. Workers often remained loyal to their employers; their attitudes were individualistic and often deferential. They accepted the *status quo* and so endorsed existing institutions - the monarchy, Parliament - and also the notion that a representative Parliament was the best protector of their interests. Although socialism seemed to offer a solution to economic problems, workers did not empathise with its political aims. This was partly due to the fact that 'a libertarian pattern of industrial relations obstructed that sense of fear and resentment which was so characteristic of workers' attitudes on the continent'.[6] In other words, unlike Europe, where workers experienced coercion and fear as part of governments' policies of maintaining stability, industrial relations in Britain were more harmonious because governments had managed to satisfy many of the trade union concerns regarding economic issues.

It could be argued that for a considerable majority within the working class that political activity was minimal. They largely rejected the doctrine of socialism and its call for collectivist politics. Hence they saw no need to withdraw their traditional respect for existing institutions. These enduring attitudes ensured both the survival of the class system and of a liberal parliamentary government. Given this conservative environment, one can appreciate not only why the eventual party was distinctly moderate in terms of socialist ideology, but also why it took so long for such a party to emerge.

c) Political Independence for the Working Class

In what circumstances did independent labour representation develop? As already demonstrated, a number of interrelating factors helped to initiate a slow but steady process. The growth of working-class education and the promulgation of socialist ideas created a forum in which people could begin to question accepted political theories. The more strident language of socialism heightened people's awareness that maybe conventional politics had its shortcomings. Disenchantment gradually gathered momentum among the more articulate members of the labour movement as, for example, issues such as the restriction of the working day to eight hours and unemployment failed to be addressed sympathetically by either the Liberals or the Conservatives. Were governments genuinely interested in the economic needs of the workers or was politics designed, just as with education, to keep the population sufficiently content and hence subservient? Thus an alternative ideology, that of socialism, did gain converts.

There were several distinctive features which characterised the new movement. One was its rejection of confrontational politics. A different socialism from that of Hyndman would prevail, one which was strongly influenced by the socialist policies expounded in Fabian lectures and meetings. Socialist propaganda was also successfully articulated through the socialist press: Blatchford's *The Clarion* and his series of letters published under the title of *Merrie England* had a major impact. Yet this was a socialism which had its roots in liberalism. It stressed the importance of human brotherhood, and it appealed to nonconformism and temperance. It emphasised the need to work peacefully rather than through class struggle. Its appeal was due to the fact that it was prepared to highlight the economic demands of the working class vociferously and to realise those demands by promoting working-class involvement in politics.

Keir Hardie epitomised these values. His background was that of liberalism and mining, but his conviction that liberalism would continue to be dominated by middle-class interests prompted his decision to promote the cause of an independent party. In January 1893, he summoned local labour organisations to a conference in Bradford, which saw the foundation of a new party, the

Independent Labour Party (ILP).

The discussions in Bradford had significant implications for the future of socialism in Britain. In particular they illustrate the distinctive features which were to isolate the British version from the more class-ridden ideology of Continental brands. They explain the pragmatic, constitutional and moderate approach of the British. Even Ben Tillett, radical leader of the dockworkers and advocate of strike action to gain working-class objectives, allied with the voices of caution when discussing the name of the new party. The original title proposed was 'The Socialist Labour Party'. Tillett, however,

1 ... could not understand why their friends should apply the term Socialist to their party. One speaker seemed anxious to accord support to their continental brethren, but in practical democratic organisation there was nothing like this old country. ... As a trade unionist with a
5 little experience and knowledge of the Labour movement he was glad to say that if there were fifty red revolutionist parties in Germany, he would rather have the solid, progressive, matter-of-fact fighting trade unionists of England, and for that reason he desired that they should keep away from their name any term of socialism. ... He had become
10 thoroughly sick of people who bore on their foreheads 'socialism' and who were no more Socialist than Bismarck.[7]

Tillett's speech exemplifies the distinctive nature of British socialism. It demonstrates quite emphatically why Marxism failed in Britain, as clearly the working class remained hostile to the adoption of bold politics. The delegates at Bradford envisaged the permeation of socialism up through society, a policy of evolution not revolution. Perhaps their cautious approach reflected the extent to which governments had successfully indoctrinated the working class through their education policies into believing the dangers posed by socialism.

Yet the Independent Labour Party encountered immediate obstacles. All its candidates in the 1895 election, including Hardie, were defeated. Friction between the ILP and the SDF militated against a united socialist front and prevented the party from gaining wider support. Paradoxically, it was the frustrations experienced by the different strands of the labour movement which caused them to coalesce in 1900. Trade unions were thwarted by the Conservative Government's lack of interest in union grievances and exasperated by divisions within the Liberal Party over issues such as the Boer War and Ireland. Perceiving that the main parties were reluctant to augment working-class representation, the TUC was prompted to instigate an independent organisation which would oversee the election to Parliament of independent MPs. It was, therefore, the resolution at the Trades Union Congress of 1899 which triggered a special conference in London in 1900.

At this conference a resolution was passed stating:

1   That this conference is in favour of establishing a distinct Labour group
    in Parliament who shall have their own Whips and agree upon their
    policy, which must embrace a readiness to co-operate with any party
    which, for the time being, may be engaged in promoting legislation in the
5   direct interest of Labour, and be equally ready to associate themselves
    with any party in opposing measures which have an opposite tendency.[8]

With the creation of the Labour Representative Committee (LRC) in
1900 came the recognition that the working class should no longer
pin their expectations on gaining political emancipation via the established parties. Independent representation and the protection of
labour interests were now paramount objectives. However, it should
be noted that the priority was to secure sympathetic legislation for the
labour movement and that, if necessary, Labour was prepared to align
with other parties. It was not the language of a party seeking to
perpetuate the class struggle but the voice of moderate socialism
ready to compromise.

   Three years later, the Labour Representative Committee demonstrated this moderate approach. Public support for the LRC was on
the increase and the Liberals were acutely aware of the potential electoral threat to their party. Radical votes could conceivably be split
between the Liberals and the LRC, giving the Conservatives an unwelcome advantage. In 1903, Herbert Gladstone and Ramsey MacDonald
signed a secret deal, the Lib-Lab Pact, whereby they would only
present one candidate between them at elections. This bore immediate fruit at the 1906 election when 29 out of 30 unopposed LRC
candidates were elected to Parliament. This was a significant milestone for the Labour movement. For the first time, an independent
working-class party had become a political force in its own right.

d) Conclusion

In what respect had the issues of class influenced the concept of
democracy by 1906? Britain still had a restricted democracy, with
about 42 per cent of all adult males still deprived of the franchise.
Organised labour, as represented by the trade unions, was still only 15
per cent of the total work force. Although there were women trade
unionists, the democratic rights of women had barely figured in the
wider aims of the labour movement. The lack of support for radical
politics was further exemplified by the small membership of socialist
organisations. Political attitudes continued to be acquiescent, tacitly
accepting the existing parliamentary institutions on the grounds that
they represented secure and fair government. The aim was not to
overthrow the system but to gain a greater share in running it.

   Yet there had been significant, if at times imperceptible, developments. A transition was taking place in which the nineteenth century
concepts of democracy were beginning to be eroded. Whereas the

ideals of liberalism had been attractive to large sections of the population, people were more aware of its shortcomings. It was within this context that the move for independent representation had gathered momentum. The creation of an independent working-class party added a vital dimension to the practice of democracy because, in so doing, the working classes were rejecting the principles of the nineteenth century. Representation by proxy - by the intelligent middle classes - would no longer suffice. The very nature of democratic government would change as the working man's voice challenged the traditional claim of the upper and middle classes to be the 'natural rulers' of the people.

3 Gender and Democracy

The final issue which constituted a challenge to the limited democracy of the nineteenth century was that of gender. For men, the question of citizenship had revolved around the extent to which men should exercise a direct control of the country's political affairs. Great advancements were made during the nineteenth century towards accepting that most men had the ability to behave as responsible citizens. It was impossible for the progress made by one sex not to exacerbate the isolation and inequality experienced by the other.

What were the circumstances, therefore, which prompted women to question this inequality? Increasing educational opportunity in the second half of the nineteenth century was one factor which highlighted the anomalous position of women in society. Intelligent, upper- and middle-class women who were the beneficiaries of a more effective education, were frustrated by their exclusion from participation in the democratic process. In addition, legislation such as the Municipal Franchise Act of 1869 and the County Councils Act of 1888 (see page 91) highlighted the disparity between the level of local and national responsibility exercised by women. A third reason was the fact that a range of economic and social disabilities, especially in relation to women's legal status within the family, was gradually addressed. Yet this progress merely aggravated women's sense of being politically disadvantaged. Hence women sought to redress their grievances.

a) Women's Rights: Theory and Practice

The first issue to consider is why women were excluded from the programme of reform in the nineteenth century. Prevailing political philosophies offer one explanation. Society was governed by a set of laws which rejected any claim to female equality. The principle of 'virtual representation' prevailed. The MP was said to represent all the members of a community, whether or not they directly elected him. In this respect, fathers and sons could likewise represent their women folk. The idea that men were the natural representatives of women was reinforced by male attitudes that the female of the species possessed neither the energy nor the intellect to vote, and therefore could not exercise sound political judgement. It did not seem ironic to the intelligent male that the very arguments levelled against women regarding their lack of political capacity had been applied to the country's agricultural labourers who were enfranchised in 1884. The fact that these educated men were reaping the benefits of a *Victorian* age, one dominated by a successful *female* monarch, also seemed to escape their formidable male logic.

Moreover, women were consigned to live in a 'separate sphere' from that of men. The two spheres were complementary to each other, but there was no scope for a merger. Women were too malleable and easily swayed by opinions to cope with the aggressive, masculine nature of government. Thus women remained under-valued, despite providing industrialists with the advantage of a cheap workforce in the expanding factories of the Industrial Revolution.

This hypocrisy was further magnified by the conviction that middle- and upper-class women should concentrate on implementing their duties as wives and mothers. This view strengthened male prejudices that married women were infinitely superior to unmarried women. Yet by the middle of the nineteenth century this idea lacked convic-tion, especially to the 2.3 million women in 1860, out of a total of 10.3 million, who lacked a husband. Of this number, two-thirds were spin-sters and one-third widows. To them, the notion of inferiority was demeaning.

For any change to occur, there had first to be a more receptive atti-tude towards women's rights. This was slow to materialise but feminist arguments were already circulating at the time of the French Revolution. One very important contribution was Mary Wollstonecraft's *A Vindication of the Rights of Women* (1792) which, inspired by the political changes of the French Revolution, argued for legal, political and educational equality with men. She asserted that women were God's creatures and therefore merited the same rights as men. However, even the revolution in France failed to recognise the equality of women.

Some arguments were propounded in England in favour of women's suffrage, but they were often shortlived. Henry Hunt, the radical reformer, petitioned Parliament in 1832 for the right of unmarried women who possessed valid property qualifications to vote. Unswayed by such radical ideas, Parliament ensured that the 1832 Reform Act specifically enfranchised 'male' persons. Even the Chartists felt it appropriate to alter the draft of their Charter from advocating 'adult suffrage' to that of 'adult male suffrage'. In the context of the times, the female franchise was a much more radical concept than adult male suffrage.

b) The Changing Environment for Women

In what context did women begin to contest these views and why were they no longer prepared to acquiesce in a society dominated at all levels, with the exception of the monarchy, by men? Important changes for women in education, the home, the law and local politics created an environment in which both men and women began to appreciate that if Britain was to shift towards a more realistic interpretation of democracy, then there had to be some debate about the political rights of women.

The first development was in education where new, good quality education opened up opportunities for women previously denied to them. The founding of North London Collegiate School for Girls by Miss Buss, and Cheltenham Ladies College by Miss Beale, both in the 1850s, set an important precedent for girls' education. In higher education, advances were first made in London where University College admitted women in the 1830s. It was not until 1871 and 1879, however, that Cambridge and Oxford respectively accepted women, though neither granted them degrees until after the end of the First World War. With improved educational facilities, women were better equipped to pursue a more independent life, an essential prerequisite to proving that they were not unthinking appendages of men. Despite the inbuilt prejudices of men who could not bear to see their prerogatives as professionals undermined, women sought careers in teaching, the law and medicine. Well-entrenched attitudes were hard to overcome, but the long-term effect was to make women more aware of the dichotomy between their growing social status in society and their political weaknesses. It was from the ranks of the well-educated and articulate members of the middle and upper classes that the suffragist pioneers emerged.

Within the family, women had long endured second-class status. Before 1857, only the husband could sue for divorce. As for retaining the right, once married, to possess her own property, women were deemed too emotional to manage such complicated matters. The accumulative effect of this wide-ranging discrimination was to generate a very determined movement of feminists who sought to rectify these injustices.

A series of legislative reforms affecting the status of women whetted women's appetites for change, especially concerning their rights within the family (see the table on page 91). Of these, the Married Women's Property Act of 1882 and the Local Government Act of 1894 were especially important. Yet as the cause of female emancipation advanced, women felt increasingly compelled to query the logic of a political system which, whilst granting them greater responsibilities in some areas, still denied them the same political rights as men.

Legislation affecting the status of women

1869 Municipal Franchise Act
This permitted women ratepayers to vote in local elections but only if they were single.

1870 School Boards
Propertied women could vote for and serve on School Boards.

1870 Married Women's Property Act
Married women granted the right to retain personal earnings and property, plus some independent income.

1875 Poor Law Boards
Women could be Poor Law Guardians.

1882 Married Women's Property Act
Married women were entitled to hold property in their own right.

1888 County Councils
County Councils were established - women with the local franchise could vote.

1892 County Councils
Women could be elected to county councils because the word 'man' in the legislation was interpreted as including 'women' as well.

1894 Parish and District Councils
Women could serve on parish and district councils.

1894 Local Government Act
This extended the vote to married women but only if they were household occupiers in their own right, not as a result of their husbands' property.

---

c) Challenges and Tactics

How did women seek to achieve effective progress and why, after nearly 40 years of activity, had they failed to realise any of their political goals? Certainly the campaign for women's suffrage which developed after 1867 was very much part of a wider movement which sought to free women from the fetters of a male-orientated society. The growth of national interest in the issue of women's suffrage gained momentum as other restrictions on women's lives were reformed. However prevailing attitudes, especially within Parliament, ensured that the challenge to the existing practice of democracy would make no progress.

Outside Parliament the initiative was led by Lydia Becker, who became the first secretary of the Manchester Women's Suffrage Society, founded in 1867. Under her leadership, a federation of suffrage societies developed across the country, their main objective being to canvass support for a women's suffrage bill. In addition,

Becker edited the *Women's Suffrage Journal,* which enabled the societies to keep in touch with each other. After her death in 1890, Becker was succeeded by Millicent Fawcett. She subsequently became the president of the National Union of Women's Suffrage Societies (the NUWSS), which set up branches in all the major towns and cities. This nationwide network of suffrage societies proved to be very effective in enlisting support and providing a forum for discussion. At all times, the women conducted a lawful, peaceful and constitutional campaign.

Their impact on politicians was mixed. In one respect they were successful. Between 1870 and 1884, almost every year witnessed a debate in Parliament on women's suffrage and it cannot be denied that the pragmatic persistence of women like Lydia Becker helped to raise the profile of their cause. A powerful ally in these debates was the philosopher and MP, J.S. Mill. Mill's political thoughts were pertinent not only to the issue of male franchise but also to that of female franchise. His ideas were forcefully argued during the debates of 1867.

> 1 Can it be pretended that women who manage an estate or conduct a business - who pay rates and taxes, ... many of whom are responsible heads of families, and some of whom, in the capacity of schoolmistresses, teach much more than a great number of the male
> 5 electors have ever learnt - are not capable of a function of which every male householder is capable? Or is it feared that if they were admitted to the suffrage they would revolutionize the State - would deprive us of any of our valued institutions, or that we should have worse laws, or be in any way worse governed through the effect of their suffrages?[9]

Mill failed to convince enough of his contemporaries that these injustices should be rectified. Britain would still adhere to the path of evolutionary change. At least for men, therefore, progress was a reality, albeit spasmodic. For most women, progress had a different connotation. They either acquired domestic servants or became domestic servants.

The problems for the suffragists was that whilst politicians might be prepared to give their individual support to the cause, they were not yet ready to adopt it as party policy. Disraeli and his successors, Lord Salisbury and Balfour, were all privately sympathetic, but publicly other policies were deemed to be more important to the Conservative Party's interests when it came to the question of prioritising party policies.

It was the 1884 Reform Act which signalled a serious political blow for women. During the debate on the extension of the franchise, William Woodal, Liberal MP for Stoke-on-Trent, proposed an amendment that:

> For all purposes connected with, and having reference to, the right to vote at Parliamentary elections, words in the Representation of the People's Act importing the masculine gender include women.[10]

Encouraged by Gladstone, government opposition to this amendment led to its defeat by 136 votes. Sadly, Gladstone was firmly convinced that women were unsuited to party politics. His views were typical of the anti-suffrage ideas which prevailed in both main parties and which thwarted the advancement of women's political rights into the early years of the twentieth century.

The persistence of such attitudes prompted the formation of another female pressure group, the Women's Social and Political Union (WSPU) in 1903. Founded by Emmeline Pankhurst, the WSPU immediately distanced itself from the conventional approach of the NUWSS. Exasperated by repeated failures to obtain results, the WSPU proposed more radical action. They planned to confront leading Liberal politicians at public meetings with the aim of forcing them to declare their unreserved support for female suffrage on an equal basis with men, rather than pursuing further extension of the franchise. Such tactics were revealed in October 1905 when, in Manchester, WSPU supporters deliberately heckled a Liberal Party meeting, demanding a Liberal endorsement of female suffrage. The imprisonment of the protesters merely provoked further militancy which ultimately culminated in the famous pre-war suffragette campaign.

Politically, the cause of women's suffrage stood little chance of progress until there was a change of attitude and government. Just as Conservative dominance in government between 1885 and 1906 accounted for the lack of progress in the suffrage movement, so the great Liberal victory of December 1905 provided the movement with much needed impetus. It opened the doors to those determined female campaigners who were convinced that they should be granted equal political status with men. Impatient with evolution, they were to resort to direct action when facing the fundamental difficulty of convincing the all-male Parliament to give up their privileged position. Many hurdles remained on the path to democracy (see Chapter 6).

4 Conclusion

By the end of the nineteenth century, three significant developments had occurred which would be instrumental in influencing the future shape and practice of democracy. The issues of education, class and gender had challenged existing attitudes and raised awareness of current shortcomings in the political system. On the one hand, governments had followed an agenda designed, as seen in their education policies, to restrain the tide of change and to preserve both a class and gender based society. As legal, social and economic reforms made their impact, so the level of expectation for further reforms increased. Inspired by the taste of reform, people at the grass roots increasingly took the initiative in order to enhance their chances of being involved in the democratic process.

To what extent, though, were these issues influential in determining the development of democracy? Through their educational policies, governments had perpetuated the influence of the upper and middle classes. However, the idea that social conditioning would enable the governing classes to maintain the *status quo* proved fallacious. It was impossible to hold back the tide of progress once universal education had begun. A subservient society would not remain politically content for long once it possessed the means to challenge inequalities. Improved educational facilities were, therefore, just one factor contributing to the changing face of democracy in Britain. The unanswered question was just how long would it take for the economic and social advances to be matched by more effective political power?

The readiness of the working classes to instigate change was another important development. As the working classes became more conscious of the extent to which existing parties neglected their interests so they sought independent working-class representation, first through the trade union movement and then through an independent political party. The latter became the prerequisite to promoting their interests.

The third challenge was that of women's franchise. Indeed, there could be no thorough breakthrough in the practice of democracy unless the participation of women was accepted. Although women were not enfranchised until 1918, the seed of reform was sown in the nineteenth century. Education, as with the working classes, gave women the opportunities to question and challenge their restricted position in society. Once concessions had been granted, it was impossible to restrain the expectations for further and more significant reforms. It was a hallmark of the suffragists' success that, despite all the setbacks in Parliament, their cause was one which would feature prominently on the political agenda after 1906.

As the era of the twentieth century began to dawn, many questions remained unresolved. If there was a substantial desire for change emanating from the grass-roots, was the challenge sufficient to constitute a serious threat to the *status quo*? Although there was class conflict in Britain, the manner in which the Labour Party developed was not indicative of a country on the verge of violent confrontation. It is important to appreciate, therefore, that whilst the new earnest members of the Labour Party used the language of socialism, the means by which they expected to realise their hopes was through the established democratic system. A belief in evolutionary change governed their tactics.

This partly explains the measured steps towards the implementation of full democracy in Britain. Yet the absence of any sense of urgency can also be attributed to other factors. Throughout the nineteenth century the political system had demonstrated a considerable degree of flexibility. The more liberal-minded members of the establishment had encouraged political, social and economic reforms whilst still maintaining their political influence over their subjects. Thus the former had retained their position of authority without any major upheaval, whilst the latter experienced material improvements in their lives. In addition, a strong sense of confidence in the country's institutions and in the concept of a limited parliamentary democracy still prevailed. As increasing numbers were deemed to be responsible citizens and were granted the vote, there seemed little reason to seek conflict with those in power. It was, therefore, the survival of liberalism as an attractive political philosophy until the outbreak of the First World War which ensured that, even at the grass-roots, the aspirations of the people would be realised within the existing political framework.

References

1 *Hansard's Parliamentary Debates*, 3rd Series, vol.CXCIX, 17 February 1870 col.465.
2 W.D. Handcock (ed), *English Historical Documents*, volXII (2) 1874-1914 (Eyre and Spottiswoode, 1977), p.520.
3 *Hansard's Parliamentary Debates*, 4th Series, 2 Edward VII, vol.CV, 24 March 1902, col.868.
4 Brian Simon, *Education and the Labour Movement 1870-1920* (Lawrence and Wishart, 1965), p.24.
5 E.H. Hunt, *British Labour History 1815-1914* (Weidenfeld and Nicolson, 1981), p.315.
6 Ross McKibbin, 'Why Was There No Marxism in Great Britain?' *English Historical Review*, 1984, XCIX, p.324.
7 *The Times*, 14 January 1893.
8 Cited in G.D.H. Cole, *British Working Class Politics* (Routledge, 1941), p.158.
9 *Hansard's Parliamentary Debates*, 3rd Series, vol.CCLXXXVII, 20 May 1867, col.818.
10 *Hansard's Parliamentary Debates*, 3rd Series, vol.CCLXXXIX, 12 June 1884, col.92.

Answering essay questions on 'Education, Labour and Women, 1868-1906'

1. How successful were politicians in managing the dangers of democracy between 1868 and 1906?
2. To what extent did education policies encourage or discourage the growth of democracy in Britain after 1867?
3. Why did it take so long for an independent working-class political party to emerge in Britain?
4. To what extent was Britain a democratic country at the end of the nineteenth century?
5. 'Second-class citizens'. How far does this statement reflect the position of women in late Victorian society?

Hints and advice: The conclusion to an essay is often the most difficult section to write and is frequently the most neglected, especially in exams. It is important to pace yourself so that you leave sufficient time to write your final paragraph.

The main purpose of your conclusion is to sum up your arguments, bringing together key points already discussed and providing a final answer to the question. If the question asked for an assessment, such as 'to what extent', make sure that you give your judgement now. Your comments should seem logical and relevant if the main section has been well argued. If you have reached a valid conclusion which suggests a different interpretation to that raised by the question, do not be afraid to put your final views. This must, however, be consistent with what you have already written.

At all costs, you must avoid including new evidence or ideas in the conclusion. Likewise do not introduce your argument in the conclusion, having mainly described events in the rest of the essay.

Consider the above questions. Question 1 will have required a broad analysis of different issues. The conclusion will need a final assessment on how successful each issue - education, management of the working class, denial of political rights to women - was in managing democracy. The phraseology of the question even suggests that politicians were possibly not successful in their goals. Your final sentences must provide your judgement. Question 3 sought an analysis of different causal factors. The conclusion here will need to sum up these points, with an emphasis on the key issues raised.

Summary Diagram

Education, Labour and Women, 1868-1906

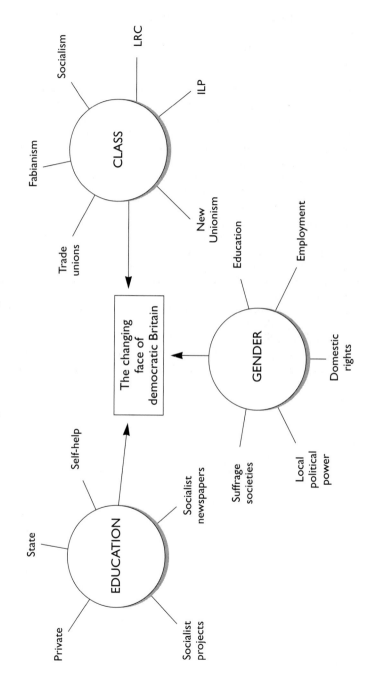

6 The Emergence of a Modern Democratic System

The modern democratic political system matured during the twentieth century. The liberal democracy which was characteristic of parliamentary government in Britain was shaped by the interaction of different, fluctuating political, social and economic forces prevalent throughout the nineteenth century. During that evolutionary process, existing political philosophies had been modified and re-evaluated. They had been forced to adjust, responding to external and internal influences as well as initiating change. As we saw in Chapters 4 and 5, political parties played a central role in determining the direction of political ideas. Likewise, they were compelled to accept that they were no longer dealing with an acquiescent electorate. The will of a significant percentage of the population could now be expressed through the ballot box. Political behaviour changed. Consequently, more responsive and democratically accountable governments emerged.

These factors paved the way for further political reform. Yet the principle of full universal suffrage was realised in piecemeal fashion, each stage achieved with little fanfare apart from the historic event of women voting for the first time in 1918. Likewise, only the suffragette campaign bore any resemblance to the fervour of the nineteenth-century radical reform movements.

If the acquisition of full universal suffrage was a haphazard process, what were the other distinguishing features of twentieth-century British democracy? The existing political framework survived, but not without a serious challenge to the constitution. Between 1910 and 1911, the House of Lords defied the Common's authority, resulting in a redefinition of the powers of the Upper House. The consolidation of the Commons' executive role was an important advance in securing democratic government.

The other major aspect of the modern democratic system was the emergence of class-based politics. The Liberal Party's hopes that they could advance a political philosophy which superseded class divisions was short-lived. Although there is continued disagreement amongst historians as to when the working class abandoned the Liberals, no one can dispute the cataclysmic effect which the First World War had on the structure of British politics. The rise of the Labour Party, in tandem with the decline of the Liberals, was accelerated by the events of 1914-18. In the post-war era, consensus politics prevailed but now policies were dominated by the ideas of conservatism and socialism. One final point must be noted. Despite differences of interpretation, the two main political parties which presided over British twentieth-century government shared the same democratic philosophy. What triumphed in the twentieth century was a combination of collectivist ideas and individualism. It was essentially a liberal philosophy, flexible enough to accommodate particular party policies but also sufficiently secure to ensure the survival of liberal democracy, especially when confronted by the gravest challenge to democracy, fascism.

1 The Final Road to Universal Suffrage, 1906-69

In 1906, Britain was still a restricted democracy, where property determined voting rights. Franchise inequality was widespread. There was little codification of the franchise - at least seven different franchises existed such as the freeman, household, lodger and service franchise - and most of these voters had to be resident in one place for at least eighteen months in order to get on the electoral register. This discriminated against those in transient or temporary employment, with as many as one million potential voters disenfranchised as a result. Plural voting exacerbated the problem because it gave about seven per cent of the electorate the right to vote in more than one place. (For further discussion on electoral deficiencies, see Robert Pearce and Roger Stearn, *Government and Reform 1815-1918*, Hodder & Stoughton, 1994). In addition, there was the continued exclusion of women with the result that, in the census of 1911, only 29.7 per cent of the total adult population could vote. Finally, neither Conservatives nor Liberals were inclined to endorse a measure of reform which might benefit their opponents.

There were, therefore, several preconditions to reform in 1906. Political attitudes would have to be more receptive to change, accepting that there was some advantage in redressing deficiencies. The notion that property must underpin the right to vote would have to be abandoned. Finally, it would have to be acknowledged that women had the same political rights as men.

a) Adult Suffrage versus Equal Suffrage

Supporters of female suffrage faced an intractable problem. From 1897 onwards, Commons' divisions on the issue of women's suffrage regularly gained majorities. However, the bills consistently failed to reach the statute books because of subsequent obstruction in the Commons. Another problem after 1906 was the fact that the initiatives emanated from backbench MPs rather than the Liberal cabinet, which declined to prioritise reform in its legislative programme. The person deemed most guilty of sanctioning this policy was Asquith, who became Prime Minister in 1908 and who refused to allow government time to discuss issues of female suffrage. His resistance was most notable when it came to the issue of whether the government would permit amendments to suffrage bills allowing for the inclusion of female suffrage.

Nevertheless, there was a growing consensus in favour of some form of franchise reform. Most Liberals preferred the principle of adult suffrage, which held several advantages. A simplified registration system, a basic residential qualification and the abolition of plural voting would probably benefit their electoral chances. There would also be the added bonus of potentially including women.

Such a position was immensely frustrating to those seeking votes for women. The NUWSS was still endeavouring to gain majority support for female suffrage by lobbying MPs and holding peaceful demonstrations. But the WSPU became increasingly militant, resorting to methods of violence and persistent defiance of the law. Understandably, politicians objected to intimidation and repeatedly refused to give their public support. If anything, their attitudes hardened as the WSPU resorted to such drastic tactics as smashing the windows of number 10 Downing Street in 1908 and commencing the notorious hunger strike campaign in 1909. (A detailed analysis of that campaign can be found in Paula Bartley's *Access to History* book, *Votes for Women 1860-1928.*) What is of concern here is why the suffrage movement made no practical progress before 1914.

The suffragettes blamed the government. In 1911, Parliament debated a Conciliation Bill which would have enfranchised property owners, including women, with a household or a £10 occupation qualification. The government intervened, proposing their own Franchise and Registration Bill for male suffrage and conceding that amendments for female suffrage could be added. The Bill passed its second reading only to collapse when the Speaker of the Commons announced that if women's suffrage amendments were included it would so alter the nature of the bill as to necessitate the submission of a new bill. As can be seen in the WSPU cartoon (see opposite), this decision confirmed the suffragettes' perception of Asquith as the real villain, his democratic credentials a mere facade. His open hostility to the suffragettes, together with his actions over legislation in Parliament, undermined any claim that he could be a true believer in democracy.

Suffragettes argued that with such persistent sabotage of legislation, the Liberals had only themselves to blame for the ensuing destruction of public property. But how feasible was it for male politicians to concede reform in the face of coercion? Could any serious extension of the franchise be contemplated once the WPSU resorted to violent tactics? Neither politicians nor voters were receptive to intimidation. Even the supportive Labour MP, George Lansbury, lost his seat at Bow and Bromley in 1912 because working men voters disapproved of the Pankhursts' campaign. Yet failure to agree on female suffrage was due to far more complex factors. The divisions within the suffrage movement weakened its overall impact. The NUWSS was indeed successful in gaining the support of the Labour Party and in appealing to a wider social audience. Their membership

THE RIGHT DISHONOURABLE DOUBLE-FACE ASQUITH.

VOTES FOR WOMEN

Women's Social and Political Union.

4, Clement's Inn, London, W.C.

Citizen Asq—th: " Down with privilege of birth—up with Democratic rule ! "

Monseigneur Asq—th: " The rights of government belong to the aristocrats by birth—men. No liberty or equality for women ! "

A cartoon published by the Women's Social and Political Union increased whereas that of the WSPU declined. But in general, working-class voters were not sufficiently motivated to empathise with a movement whose image seemed distinctly upper- or middle-class. Even for sympathetic politicians, there was less incentive to consider female suffrage when other more urgent matters of domestic reform required attention.

The last attempts to achieve reform before the outbreak of war were W.H. Dickinson's Representation of the People Bill in 1913 and a Plural Voting Bill in March 1914. The former was defeated by 47 votes, whilst the latter was curtailed by the intervention of the war. With the commencement of the war, all immediate thought of reform was dropped.

b) The Representation of the People Act, 1918

In 1918, the most radical of all the reform acts was enacted. Modern democracy came of age, the principle of one man, one vote was now enshrined in the statute books, whilst six months' residency and an age limit of 21 were the only prerequisites for exercising this democratic right. For men, voting ceased to be a privilege. One ancient tradition had been abandoned. Another new principle was also instituted: the right, albeit still limited, of women to vote. Given the apparent indifference which plagued pre-war efforts to pass reform, what were the factors which influenced such a radical *volte-face* on behalf of the government?

Contemporary supporters of women's suffrage had no doubts about who was responsible for eroding the prejudices of an all-male Parliament. In their opinion, it was the continued pressure of the women's movement which had sustained the momentum. Christabel Pankhurst asserted that it was the possible resumption of militancy which politicians sought to avert, whilst her sister, Sylvia Pankhurst, in her book, *The Suffrage Movement* (1977), linked this fear to a broader concern about the security of a post-war Europe.

> 1 Undoubtedly the large part taken by women during the War in all branches of social service had proved a tremendous argument for their enfranchisement. Yet the memory of the old militancy, and the certainty of its recurrence if the claims of women were set aside, was a much
> 5 stronger factor in overcoming the reluctance of those who would again have postponed the settlement. The shock to the foundations of existing social institutions already reverberating from Russia across Europe, made many old opponents desire to enlist the new enthusiasm of women voters to stabilise the Parliamentary machine.[1]

There are several striking features about the above statement. It echoed the familiar strident tone of the pre-war suffragette movement which had justified the deployment of militant tactics. This approach was now vindicated as having shaped public opinion. But there was also a recognition that the patriotic role of women had been a contributory factor. Supporters of the WSPU in particular had rallied to support the war effort, their sudden endorsement of a hitherto disliked government seeming somewhat incongruous to their opponents. Finally, the reference to the situation in Europe reflected a genuine concern amongst politicians that extensive enfranchisement would counteract possible instability arising from the revolutionary upheavals in Russia.

It is clear that the war precipitated reform. Politicians were anxious that returning soldiers would be automatically disenfranchised because of the residency requirements. When the government set up the Speaker's Conference in 1916, extensive male enfranchisement was high on the agenda. The more intractable issue was female suffrage. Asquith, who ceased to be Prime Minister in December 1916, was now prepared publicly to endorse votes for women, claiming that their war efforts deserved an appropriate reward. But whilst the war had given women a prominent role in the nation's defence, underlying attitudes about the status of women were unaltered. At the conclusion of the war, women were compelled to resume their traditional domestic roles. The prevailing argument was that only mature, reliable women should get the vote. Impose an age limit of 30, and they could be more certain of enfranchising sensible voters who, if married, would probably vote the same as their husbands. Moreover, with male voters still in the majority, there would be minimum damage to the constitution. Thus, in 1918, a restricted group of women received the vote in the expectation that their induction to national politics would benefit existing institutions. As with all previous reforms, however, once the door of opportunity had edged open, it could not be shut.

c) Political Equality, 1928-69

The case for complete political equality between men and women was hardly a headline issue after 1918. Underlying fears that younger, single women would vote Labour deterred the Conservatives, whilst the Liberals, as partners in the coalition government of 1918-22, were beset with more urgent political problems. Although 40 per cent of all voters were women, government policies were tailored towards improving women's social and economic status rather than their political rights. This uncommitted attitude was a cross-party phenomenon. Hence when Baldwin, on becoming prime minister in 1924, announced a promise of equal franchise, few politicians expressed any concern at the subsequent absence of legislation.

Yet by 1928 there remained few valid arguments for denying women equal franchise. It is true that the National Union of Societies for Equal Citizenship (formally the NUWSS) maintained a high level of pressure on the government during the 1920s and was probably instrumental in persuading the government to lower the proposed age limit from 25 to 21. Nevertheless, a momentous step towards greater democracy was achieved in 1928 with the Equal Franchise Act.

Two final acts secured the current system of representation. The Representation of the People Act, 1948, abolished plural voting and the University seats - separate seats possessed by some universities. It also removed the requirement of a period of residency in order to get on the electoral register. Note that this act was passed by the first Labour government to have a majority in the House of Commons - Clement Attlee's government of 1945-50, and that it clearly removed the inherent bias of a voting system which had favoured the Conservatives.

The second act, also passed by a Labour Government, was the Representation of the People Act 1969, which reduced the voting age from 21 to 18. Since 1969, minor amendments have been passed concerned mainly with electoral expenses and postal votes, but probably the most significant development in terms of representation has been the commencement of direct elections to the European Parliament (European Assembly Elections Act 1978). We are no longer just British citizens but citizens of Europe.

2 Constitutional Reform

At the time of the French Revolution, the House of Commons struggled to establish its authority over that of the Crown. Reformers condemned an authoritarian monarchy and demanded that the will of the Commons be respected. Subsequently, a more comfortable relationship between Crown and Commons evolved, as the former ceased to interfere in the executive. But although the balance of power had shifted steadily towards the House of Commons, the authority of that institution was repeatedly challenged and thwarted by the House of Lords. The Lords could still amend or reject unpopular legislation passed by the Commons. This veto allowed the Lords to retain a significant role in determining the success of legislation. It was commonly accepted, however, that money bills would not be obstructed because failure to approve government finances would render the government impotent. Nevertheless, in the nineteenth century the Lords frequently deployed their constitutional rights such as during the 1832 Reform Bill crisis and over Home Rule.

In 1906, the Liberals had a Commons majority of 243 seats and sought to enact radical legislation as part of a programme of domestic reform. Several bills soon suffered, defeated by the opposition of the Lords. Yet such actions raised a serious constitutional question. What right did a select and unrepresentative group of people have to override the democratic wishes of the people who had given it a mandate to implement certain policies? It became only a matter of time before a conflict of 'peers' versus 'people' would erupt.

Several issues have to be examined when analysing the crisis. Firstly, what provoked the crisis? Secondly, what were the key constitutional questions? Finally, what was the significance of the House of Lords crisis in terms of establishing greater democracy in Britain?

a) The Cause: the People's Budget, 1909

In 1909, Lloyd George, Chancellor of the Exchequer, introduced his famous 'People's Budget'. The thrust of the budget was to raise taxes to fund social reform in Britain. The most obvious target for increased taxation was the aristocracy, whose untaxed wealth had enabled them to retain an influence within the country far out of proportion with their numbers. Increases in income tax, death duties, a tax on unearned increment, tobacco and spirits provoked indignant outrage amongst their lordships, who viewed the motives of the government as being intentionally vindictive towards their class. Convinced that such a deliberate attack must be repelled, the Lords broke the unwritten convention that they should never reject a money bill and defeated the bill in the Lords in November 1909 by a margin of 275 votes. (For detailed discussion of the Budget crisis and the House of Lords crisis, see R. Pearce and R. Stearn, *Government and Reform 1815-1918.*)

Was this conflict predictable? At a speech at the Annual Meeting of the National Liberal Federation at Liverpool on 24 May 1906, Lloyd George made the following comments:

1 What is the House of Commons? The House of Commons represents forty-one millions of people. There is not a man who tills the soil; there is not a man who works in a factory; there is not a man who goes to an office in this city; there is not a man who goes down into the deeps of
5 the earth to bring up its treasures for the benefit of mankind; there is not a man who sails the ocean from British ports; there is not a man who gives brain, muscle, time, energy, thought to the industries that make up the wealth, the strength, the prosperity, the might of this land, who has not a voice and a vote in sending a man to the House of
10 Commons. The House of Commons represents the industry of the country. What does the House of Lords represent? It represents the idleness of the country ...
    What about the House of Lords? There is not a workman there.... Four-fifths of the people of this country absolutely unrepresented in
15 that House.... They are not men who are there because of any special gifts, but purely from the accident of their birth.[2]

This scornful invective was just one of several attacks by Lloyd George against the unfair privileges of the Lords. As evidence of the undemocratic behaviour of the Lords accumulated, Lloyd George presented the Budget crisis as a confrontation forced upon the Liberals by an unrepresentative and insolent assembly. In addition, the Conservatives were resorting to their natural majority in the Lords to

---

Events 1909-11

30 November 1909	Lords rejected the Budget.
December 1909	Asquith called a general election seeking a mandate for complete authority over finance bills and the abolition of the Lords' veto.
January 1910	Election: Libs=274; Cons=272; Irish Nationalists=82; Labour=40
March 1910	Parliament Bill introduced. Main proposals: abolish the Lords' power to amend or veto a finance bill - all other bills could only be delayed for two years after which they became law. Lifetime of Parliament reduced from seven to five years.
28 April 1910	Lords passed the Budget.
6 May 1910	Death of Edward VII.
June to November 1910	Constitutional Conference sought compromise. Ended in deadlock.
16 November 1910	George V gave secret pledge to Asquith to use his royal prerogative and to create new Liberal peers if the Lords defeated the Parliament Bill.
28 November 1910	Parliament dissolved with aim of seeking fresh approval for reform of Lords.
December 1910	Election: Libs=272; Cons=272; Irish Nationalists=84; Labour=42
February 1911	Parliament Bill introduced again to Commons
May 1911	House of Commons approved the Bill.
July 1911	Bill debated in House of Lords. Large number of amendments drastically altered composition of the Bill. Amendments rejected by House of Commons; details of King's pledge revealed.
9-10 August 1911	Final debate in House of Lords. Bill accepted by 131 to 114 votes.

---

defeat unwelcome legislation because they could not overcome the Liberal majority in the Commons.

Asquith provided further insights into the Liberals' sense of exasperation with the Lords when he spoke at the Royal Albert Hall on 11 Decembe, 1909.

1 … neither I nor any other Liberal Minister supported by a majority in the House of Commons is going to submit again to the rebuffs and humiliations of the last four years. We shall not assume office and we shall not hold office unless we can secure the safeguards which experi-

5 ence shows us to be necessary for the legislative utility and honour of
   the party of progress ... We are not proposing the abolition of the
   House of Lords or setting up a single Chamber, but we do ask, and we
   are going to ask, the electors to say that the House of Lords shall be
   confined to the proper functions of a second Chamber. The absolute
10 veto which it at present possesses must go.... the people in future when
   they elect a new House of Commons, must be able to feel what they
   cannot feel now, that they are sending to Westminster men who will have
   the power not merely of proposing and debating, but of making laws.[3]

The Lords' veto of the Budget was the green light to proceed with
constitutional reform. It was a blatant affront to democracy to have
the will of the people undermined by a select and unrepresentative
assembly. The Lords' veto had to be abolished.

b) The Constitutional Crisis

The key question was how to negotiate such a bill past the expected
opposition of the second house. The only solution, as in 1832, would
be to seek the King's co-operation to create sufficient Liberal peers,
thereby overruling the Conservative majority in the Lords. But it was
soon apparent that the King's consent would only be considered if
Asquith first appealed to the country. Even then, it is unclear whether
Edward VII was prepared to proceed with the destruction of the
House of Lords.

Unfortunately the election results of January 1910 compounded
the government's problems because the balance of power resided in
the hands of two minority parties: the Irish and Labour. John
Redmond, leader of the Irish Nationalists, seized the advantage and
made his party's support conditional on two issues: the enactment of
Home Rule and the abolition of the Lords' veto. The opposition
immediately accused the government of succumbing to Redmond's
revolutionary tactics. They also alleged that the Liberals were abusing
their authority in order to abolish the Second Chamber and to secure
the complete domination of the House of Commons. The Liberals
likewise blamed the Conservatives for unconstitutional behaviour.
Asquith protested against the manipulation of a Conservative
majority, either in the Commons or in the Lords, to thwart anti-
Conservative legislation. The battleground was graphically depicted
by the two contrasting cartoons on pages 108 and 109. The first
appeared in a Liberal publication, *The Westminster Gazette*, on 10
February 1910. The second was published by *The Conservative and
Unionist* in June 1910. One reflected the perception of blatant disre-
gard for democracy, the other, one of betrayal and deception.

The complicated events of the constitutional crisis can be traced in
the table on page 106. They culminated in a tense debate on 9-10
August 1911, during which the Ditchers, those prepared to resist all

THE LORDS AND THE PEOPLE.

A cartoon published in The Westminster Gazette, 10 February 1910

THE SERPENT IN THE EGG.

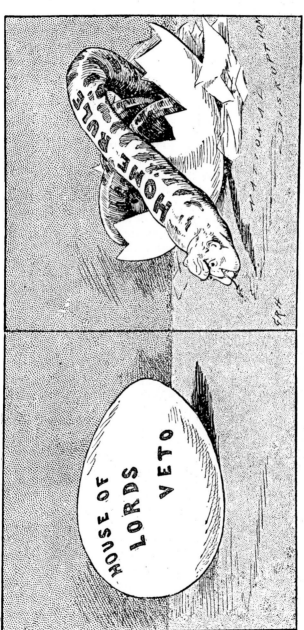

"This question of the Veto is the supreme issue for us. It means Home Rule for Ireland."—
Mr. John Redmond, M.P., Liverpool, March 20, 1910.

A cartoon published in The Conservative and Unionist, *June 1910*

change, and the Hedgers, those who were more realistic and ready to compromise on a reduction of power, argued passionately for their respective views. Against cries of 'traitors' and 'rats', the government, supported by 37 Unionist peers and 13 Bishops, finally curtailed the powers of the House of Lords by a majority of just 17.

c) Outcome

What were the implications of the Parliament Act for democracy in Britain? Some important constitutional issues had clearly been addressed. The balance of power was now consolidated in the House of Commons. An absolute veto had been replaced by a delaying veto, the justification for the latter being that it gave the incumbent government time to reflect on and even alter the proposed legislation. But the authority of the House of Commons could not be subordinated to that of the Lords.

The Act also removed the problem of the Conservatives exploiting their majority in the Lords to their advantage. The right of a democratically elected party to implement a particular set of policies was endorsed, whatever their political persuasion. This was an acceptance that the people, through the ballot box, were entitled to make their political choice and, that once given, their rulers had a duty to carry out that mandate. It could not be overruled by a minority. Finally, by reducing the lifetime of Parliament from seven to five years, the Act ensured that representatives became more accountable to the electorate. It was easier to dismiss an MP who ignored the interests of his constituents.

However, a number of anomalies remained. In the preamble to the 1911 Parliament Act, there was a specific declaration to 'substitute for the House as it at present exists a Second Chamber constituted on a popular rather than a hereditary basis.'[4] This was never implemented despite the fact that, even during the crisis, the Tory Lord Lansdowne had proposed a thorough review of the Lords' composition. The failure to adopt radical reform was perhaps governed by a realisation that an elected second chamber could complicate and challenge the authority of the Commons. Thus Britain was left with a House of Lords in which, even today, over 60 per cent of those eligible to attend do so because of their birthright. The remainder are lifetime peers, first created as a result of the 1958 Life Peerages Act. It should be noted that in 1911 the first act granting payments to MPs was enacted, precisely in order to facilitate the integration of working-class representatives into Parliament. The concept that privilege based on landed wealth was an appropriate qualification for government had finally been rebuffed. Yet juxtaposed with a more democratic House of Commons was an undemocratic second chamber. If its function was to restrain and modify the acts of the lower chamber, it was surely incongruous for it to remain an unelected body.

3 Political Philosophies

Although Britain had not achieved full democracy by 1906, it was being increasingly recognised that all interest groups had a stake in government - in sharp contrast to the situation in the eighteenth century when only narrow interests were represented. A key concern of those in or seeking power was how to address the interests of the working-class electorate. Should policies be designed which catered for their particular class needs or should their interests be subsumed into those of the whole nation? The Liberals were swayed by the philosophies of Hobhouse and Hobson whose vision of State collectivism (see pages 62-64) was designed to address inequality and avoid class conflict. This philosophy laid the foundations for the modern political state. But the Liberals had one inherent weakness. They failed to dispel the image of a party controlled by the upper and middle classes. It was Labour, not the Liberals, who finally captured the working-class vote.

The Conservatives sought to retain the ethos of capitalism and free enterprise. As in the late nineteenth century, they advocated a judicious 'management' of democracy whilst still adhering to the philosophy that men were not equal. Politics was distinguished by those who could and should rule, and those who obeyed and followed. For those people alarmed by events in Russia in 1917, and by the democratisation of British politics, Conservative efforts to 'control' the masses had a strong appeal.

Finally, all these political assumptions were challenged in the twentieth century by the growing attraction of socialism. As with the Liberals, the British Labour Party perceived inequalities in society, but proposed a more interventionist style by the state in order to address the problems. Whereas liberalism clung to an essentially middle-class view of politics, Labour believed more emphatically in the direct representation of the people. Their aim was to achieve a classless society notwithstanding their pragmatic approach to socialism.

a) The Decline of Liberalism

How successful were the Liberals in attracting working-class votes? As discussed in Chapter 4, the Liberals now rejected the nineteenth-century concept that each individual was responsible for his own welfare, that poverty was the fault of the individual. Politics had to become more responsive and humane.

Their answer was a programme of extensive reforms of which the 1906 Workers' Compensation Act, 1908 Old Age Pensions Act, 1909 Trade Boards Act, 1911 National Insurance Act, 1912 Minimum Wage Act for Miners and 1913 Trade Union Act were notable examples. The controversial People's Budget of 1909 began a process of legitimising the use of taxes to alleviate poverty.

What were the motives behind the Liberals' legislative programme? Although the intention was to embark on a programme of welfare reform, the measures were not envisaged as constituting far-reaching socialist policies. Radical policies were tempered with traditional Liberal policies, 'New Liberalism' was countered by 'Old Liberalism', such as support for the disestablishment of the Church in Wales. Electoral support in middle-class areas had to be retained as much as working-class support encouraged. What is disputable, however, is whether these policies successfully enabled the Liberals to preserve working-class support throughout the pre-war period. Was liberalism healthy enough to transcend class differences? Or can it be argued that, with democratisation, the Liberal Party failed to make the transition necessary both in policies and style to remain a party with mass appeal?

One school of thought is that the Liberals' successful amalgamation of old and new ideas produced a flourishing and active party which was far from collapse in 1914. These policies enabled the party to retain the crucial support of both the working class and the middle class right up to the outbreak of war. This thesis would suggest that class politics had not yet become a significant factor in determining political allegiances, and that the Liberals had overcome potential problems of class tension. According to Trevor Wilson, the eventual downfall of the Liberals was not because it lacked intellectual direction, but because it was unable to adjust to the constraints of war.

An alternative viewpoint is that the Liberals failed to respond adequately to sectional class interests whereas Labour was poised to exploit the working-class vote. However, because Labour was unfairly disadvantaged by a high level of disenfranchisement amongst the working class, its electoral weaknesses seemed disproportionately greater prior to 1914. Once the electorate trebled in 1918, Labour could assume its natural place in the execution of democratic government.

Whatever the underlying causes, it cannot be denied that by 1918 Labour had replaced the Liberals as the second largest political party. Forced to negotiate a coalition government with the Conservatives in 1915, followed by the ideological split between supporters of Lloyd George and Asquith in 1916, the Liberal Party never recovered its former electoral strength. Traditional Liberals accused Lloyd George of betraying liberalism, selling its principles such as freedom of the individual for the sake of conscription in 1916. By 1918 radical Liberals no longer had a party which represented their ideology. The coalition Liberals were too tightly associated with a range of policies resembling those of the Conservative Party. The only alternative was to defect to the party most able to defend their principles. As Martin Pugh has claimed:

> Ultimately the war entailed not an intellectual or programmatic outflanking of one party by the other so much as the inheritance by Labour of the broad ground of pre-1914 Progressivism.[5]

Despite defections to both the Conservatives and Labour, it was not immediately obvious that the Liberals faced imminent collapse. In 1923, they reunited as a party under the banner of free trade, but ultimately they could not overcome the handicap of being the third party in British politics. By 1935 the party was reduced to an insignificant, minor party, its only legacy to British politics being one of strong Liberal principles.

b) The Survival of Conservatism

In 1906, the Conservative Party faced the unpalatable truth. It was in opposition for the first time in 20 years. The story of the Conservative Party in the pre-war period is of a party split over the relative merits of protectionism and weakened by political in-fighting. Balfour's inability to provide strong leadership merely prolonged the factional divisions. The impression given was of a party preoccupied with its internal problems, rather than a party seeking to reach out to the electorate. The party's policy of obstructing Liberal legislation in the House of Lords compounded the image of a party unable to accept democracy and which preferred the values of the past.

Between 1909 and 1914, the Conservatives' reaction to two crises confirmed the above profile. As well as the House of Lords' battle, Conservatives were confronted with the prospect of Irish Home Rule. Unable to veto Home Rule legislation and appalled at the thought that Unionists in Ireland would now be betrayed, Conservatives resorted to unprecedented tactics. Bonar Law, who had replaced Balfour as leader in 1911, fuelled the impending conflict in Ireland by offering direct endorsement of Protestant resistance:

> I can imagine no length of resistance to which Ulster can go on which I should not be prepared to support them, and which, in my belief, they would not be supported by the overwhelming majority of the British people.[6]

Underpinning Bonar Law's statement was an inherent belief in the importance of maintaining the Empire and its union with the United Kingdom. It reflected continuity with past policies but also suggested yet again that the Conservatives were undemocratic. The aspirations of Catholics were immaterial because what mattered most was to uphold the principles of a constitution which was governed by Protestantism.

It was the First World War which arrested the decline of the Conservatives, enabling them to emerge from the war stronger and more united. Firstly, the wartime experience of office enhanced their authority nationally. Secondly, the Conservatives were more comfortable with promoting nationalism and patriotism than the Liberals. Thus the Conservatives could exploit the emotions engendered by war to their advantage without risking the agonised soul-searching present within the Liberal Party. Thirdly, they could reverse the pre-war damage to their reputation by highlighting the dangers of militancy and extremism within the Labour Party, as well as that of communism in Russia. Having suffered from sectionalism and a narrow outlook, the Conservatives were now preparing themselves for a more realistic approach to twentieth-century politics.

The opportunity to test the changing Conservative Party arose in 1922 when, at a meeting in the Carlton Club on 22 October 1922, backbench Conservatives voted to withdraw their support for Lloyd George's coalition government. This decision had profound consequences for the future direction of British politics. It left the coalition Liberals isolated, still alienated from Asquithian Liberals. It signalled a return to two-party politics, now dominated by the Conservatives and Labour. The Conservatives soon enjoyed a new hegemony in British politics, only briefly interrupted during the next 40 years by Labour Governments in 1924, 1929-31 and 1945-51.

So what was distinctive about the style of Conservative politics in the post-war era? Did the Conservatives make any noticeable concessions to a democratic electorate? One important shift in Conservative ideology was a more sincere respect for the electorate and parliamentary democracy. Previously, Conservatives had tolerated democratic reform, their motives influenced more by pragmatism than belief. Now their pervasive fear of the working classes finally dissipated as Conservatives appreciated that it was possible to appeal to the sensible and moderate members of the working class.

Under Baldwin, party leader from 1923 to 1937, conservatism became distinctly nondoctrinal. Baldwin understood both the importance of reaching out to a broad constituency and of resisting strong, sectional-based politics. He offered the electorate common-sense policies such as low government expenditure and *laissez-faire* economic policies. Women were encouraged to become Conservative voters with policies which reiterated the value of their domestic life. Propaganda images promoted the 'home' and 'hearth', whereas feminism and socialism allegedly denigrated the role of women. In addition, conservatism had to be humanitarian in order to maintain a sense of common purpose amongst all sectors of society. In a key policy speech, Baldwin said:

> 1 I want to see the spirit of service to the nation the birthright of every
> member of the Unionist party - Unionist in the sense that we stand for
> the Union of these two nations of which Disraeli spoke two generations
> ago; union among our own people to make one nation of our own
> 5 people at home ...[7]

In many respects there was continuity with the past, with values that depicted the unchanging nature of being English. The long-standing image of conservatism as being a comfortable, non-antagonistic philosophy persisited. Just as the Primrose League had performed a vital social function, so village fetes, whist drives and afternoon teas enabled those anxious to retain their comfortable urban or rural life to adhere to a set of values which did not undermine their sense of security. In one sense, the rhetoric and the philosophies had not changed since the time of Disraeli. The combination of traditional and more modern ideas created a stable and reliable party. Indeed, it has been suggested that fascism did not secure a large following in Britain because of the Conservative Party. In Europe, however, the lack of an equivalent party left potential conservative supporters attracted to more extreme politics.

c) The Rise of Labour

In 1906, the Labour Party was a minority force in British politics. By 1918, it had ousted the Liberal Party to become the party with the second highest popular vote, although it was not yet recognised as the official opposition. By the end of the next decade, Labour had twice held office, albeit as a minority government each time. Was this meteoric rise symptomatic of fundamental changes in political behaviour in Britain? Did it indicate that with greater democracy, the radical politics of the nineteenth century were no longer able to satisfy the expectations of the twentieth century? Did Labour offer a political philosophy which was distinctive and more appropriate to the needs of a mass electorate?

Labour was not ideally placed to assume the mantle of a radical party. The 1903 Lib-Lab Pact had been a significant milestone in furthering working-class representation but it hindered Labour's ability to strike out independently. Throughout the pre-war period, Labour was hampered by a number of factors. The Liberals held the initiative in determining policies and Labour could scarcely dissent from supporting radical reforms. Labour MPs were inevitably inexperienced politicians, and often inarticulate in debates when faced by such heavyweights such as Lloyd George and Winston Churchill. Also, the Parliamentary Labour Party, its official title after 1906, was a mouthpiece for a range of socialist groups: conservative trade unions, co-operative societies, the Fabian Society and the more radical Independent Labour Party. All were affiliated members, but consensus was a difficult goal. Finally, despite a surge between trade union activity in 1910 and 1914, the working classes showed little inclination to seek out and embrace a new radical political allegiance.

The First World War, however, was a major factor in accelerating changes in political behaviour. This, combined with the 1918 Representation of the People Act, had a momentous influence on the future direction of democracy in Britain. By 1918, Labour had severed its links with the Liberals and, complete with a distinct set of policies, was poised to become a major participant in politics.

The war assisted Labour in several ways. Labour was invited to join the coalition governments of Asquith in 1915 and Lloyd George in 1916. Labour's pre-war leader, Ramsey MacDonald, had resigned from the parliamentary party in objection to the war, leaving Arthur Henderson to assume the leadership. Henderson gained invaluable experience as a Cabinet minister, and both he and his colleagues could thereby prove to their sceptics that Labour could be trusted in government. However, it was Henderson's dismissal from the Cabinet in 1917, over Labour's support for an international socialist peace conference in Stockholm, which was more significant for Labour's future development.

Labour had to divest itself of its image as a political lap-dog. Foreseeing the enormous changes ahead once war was over, Labour formulated two crucial documents: a constitution and a key policy statement. The constitution was significant because it ensured that Labour did not become a dogmatic, narrow-focused socialist party. It diluted the influence of trade unions and other socialist groups by permitting individual membership. On the other hand, it also committed the party to socialist principles whilst adeptly avoiding the word 'socialism'. The party's aim was:

1 To secure for the producers by hand or by brain the full fruits of their industry, and the most equitable distribution thereof that may be possible, upon the basis of the common ownership of the means of production and the best obtainable system of popular administration
5 and control of each industry or service.[8]

Thus potential moderate Labour sympathisers were not alienated by a direct reference to socialism. The second document, *Labour and the New Social Order*, established the foundations of Labour policy for the next 30 years, emphasising above all the importance of the democratic control of society.

Yet in reality, what did Labour offer the electorate during the inter-war years? On the one hand, there was a clear theoretical commitment to socialist policies such as nationalisation of industry and a national minimum wage. On the other hand, Labour provided few constructive policies to deal with the economic crises of the 1930s. MacDonald's determination to present an acceptable face of socialism finally cost him his membership of the Labour Party, whose members could not forgive him for being prepared to head a National Government in 1931. In their view, his actions were prompted by personal rather than party interests.

Several factors militated against a concerted implementation of socialism by Labour during the inter-war years. Firstly, Labour governments were hampered by the lack of a parliamentary majority. Secondly, the realities of gaining power and the need to prove their respectability made Labour politicians cautious. Finally, Labour was determined to dispel public fears about links with communism. As Labour matured into being the second major political party in

Britain, it deliberately shunned the stigma of revolution showing respect for parliamentary democracy and the policies of co-operation. The failure of the 1926 General Strike added impetus to this aim, as well as convincing trade unionists that they would have to work through Parliament. Labour's policies were nonconfrontational whilst still endeavouring to enhance the role of the State.

4 Conclusion

The twentieth century saw a continuation of the democratic processes commenced in the late eighteenth century. These ultimately culminated in universal suffrage. What were the factors which finally determined the achievement of full democracy?

Democracy had evolved in a haphazard fashion, influenced by a range of factors. Acceptance of democratic principles was far from universal. Indeed it could be argued that politicians were never intrinsically democratic. Rather, as had occurred in the nineteenth century, they had come to terms with changing economic and social conditions which highlighted the anachronisms of an undemocratic political system. Striving for political advantage, politicians conceded the enlargement of the franchise in the hope that thankful voters would augment their party's fortunes. Moreover, reform was still granted in piecemeal, even in a begrudging fashion, as in the case of female suffrage in 1918. Democracy was accommodated, not because it was openly welcomed but because politicians could no longer find practical arguments with which to oppose it.

Opposition to democracy was also undermined by events such as the First World War. The war challenged the principles of pre-war Edwardian society, in particular destroying the deferential and acquiescent attitudes of the working classes. The war raised their expectations of a new Britain, one in which their political status had to be recognised. Such expectations were also the result of the long-term effects of better education as well as the more widespread dissemination of information through a popular press.

The system of democracy which developed in Britain was both tempered and partial and therefore far from perfect. In its favour, it avoided the many cataclysmic changes which affected political reform elsewhere in Europe. It had created a form of democracy which has proven resilient to the extremes of the twentieth century. At the same time, several anomalies prevailed. The reform of the House of Lords was a pragmatic response to a particular crisis. It was not the product of a fundamental redesign of the British constitution. It left Britain with a weakened but still undemocratic second house. Therefore, although Britain can claim to be democratic because she possesses universal suffrage and a modern, multi-party political system, whether Britain has really implemented full democracy remains questionable.

References
1   E.S. Pankhurst, *The Suffrage Movement* (Virago, 1977), pp.607-8.
2   David Lloyd George, *The Government and Its Work* (The Liberal Publication Department, 1906), pp.7-8.
3   *The Times*, 11 December 1909, cited in Kenneth O. Morgan, *The Age of Lord George* (George Allen and Unwin Ltd, 1971), p.149.
4   Cited in F.F. Ridley and Michael Rush (eds), *British Government and Politics since 1945: Changes in Perspective* (Oxford University Press, 1995), p.225.
5   Martin Pugh, *The Making of Modern British Politics 1867-1939, 2nd edn* (Blackwell, 1993), p.216.
6   Cited in Paul Adelman, *Great Britain and the Irish Question 1800-1922* (Hodder & Stoughton, 1996), p.123.
7   Cited in John Ramsden, *The Age of Balfour and Baldwin 1902-1940* (Longman, 1978), p.210.
8   *The Labour Party Constitution*, 20 February 1918 (Co-operative Printing Society Ltd, 1918), p.4.

Source-based questions on 'The Emergence of a Modern Democratic System'

1. The House of Lords Crisis: Lloyd George and Asquith

Read the two extracts by Lloyd George and Asquith on pages 105 and 106-7. Answer the following questions:

a) What contrasting images of the two Houses of Parliament did Lloyd George portray? (3 marks)

b) Does Lloyd George give an accurate description of democracy in Britain in his comments? (3 marks)

c) What did Asquith (lines 2-3) mean by the 'rebuffs and humiliations of the last four years'? (2 marks)

d) Using your knowledge, explain how Asquith's understanding of 'the proper functions of a Second Chamber' differed from the opinion held by the House of Lords. (5 marks)

e) How useful are these documents in helping us to understand the subsequent House of Lords crisis? (7 marks)

2. The House of Lords Crisis: Cartoons from The Westminster Gazette and The Conservative and Unionist

Examine carefully these cartoons on pages 108 and 109 and answer the following questions.

a) Explain the title of the cartoon from *The Conservative and Unionist*. (3 marks)

b) Study the cartoon from *The Westminster Gazette*. What comments about the House of Lords was the cartoonist attempting to convey? (5 marks)

c) With reference to both cartoons and using your own knowledge, comment on the reliability of these cartoons as evidence of the House of Lords crisis. (7 marks)

Summary Diagram
The Emergence of a Modern Democratic System

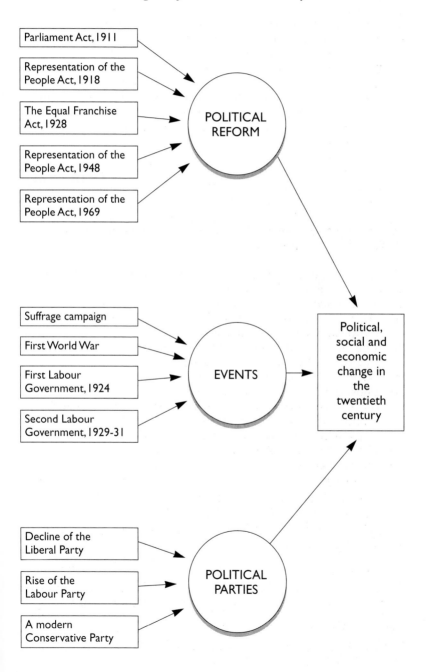

7 A Modern Democracy?

In Chapter 1, this book outlined the many imperfections of parliamentary government which prevailed at the end of the eighteenth century. Subsequent chapters have analysed the process of change which ensued over the next 200 years and which culminated in the modern democratic system with which we are now familiar. What have been the main characteristics of the emergence of democracy during this period and how did they come about? What are the strengths of British democracy? What are its imperfections, and what room is there for possible further reform?

1 The Characteristics of the Growth of Democracy

The growth of democracy in Britain was distinguished by two related developments. The first was the broadening of the franchise to universal suffrage. The second was that politics was transformed from representing narrow sectional interests to that of majority interests.

a) The Broadening of the Franchise

One major reason for the establishment of parliamentary democracy was the gradual rationalisation and reform of the franchise. In the eighteenth century, a restricted and diverse form of franchise existed, resulting in a totally undemocratic Parliament. The franchise was determined by the possession of private property because that was considered to be the natural guarantee of political security and of good government. Inevitably, the people deemed most capable of exercising political responsibility were members of the landed classes. Little did they imagine how much would be conceded over the next 200 years. Why did this aristocratic monopoly of power become untenable?

Given the momentous economic and social changes arising from the Industrial Revolution, it was, in retrospect, not surprising that political reform was granted. Contemporaries, however, did not act with a sense of political vision. Those responsible for reform were not great democrats but members of the establishment, keen to minimise the influence of the masses for as long as possible. Each act of reform - the enfranchisement of the middle classes (1832), the urban working classes (1867), the agricultural workers (1884) and finally women (1918) - was granted as a pragmatic concession rather than an intrinsic right. Yet what politicians did not appreciate was that each act left anomalies in the political system. How could any act establish a sustainable criterion for voting, when the skills, expectations and social and economic status of the electorate were in a continuous state of flux? What is clear is that politicians resisted each further expansion of the franchise for as long as possible, until logically they could no longer defend an outdated system.

It was not until 1918 that the concept of the vote as a natural right was implemented and even then it applied only to men. For women, the same attitudes that had applied to men still prevailed. They, too, had to demonstrate that female enfranchisement would not jeopardise the safe functioning of the constitution. Since full equality in 1928, governments have merely refined the franchise. It is perhaps an indication that the achievement of full democracy remains an ongoing process. Still to be resolved is the issue of whether the current voting age of 18 should be lowered to 16, the age at which young people can get married.

b) The Transformation of Politics

The second key feature of the growth of democracy was the development of a modern political system which both appealed to and represented broad sectional interests. In the eighteenth century, the distinction between the Tories and the Whigs was minimal. Both were dominated by the aristocracy and pursued policies which were tailored to their narrow interests. Patronage and corruption, uncontested elections, and a total lack of proportional representation were all notable features of politics. How did the modern political system emerge and what role did each political party play in determining the nature of British democracy?

For the Tories, accepting the progression to greater democracy was difficult. Traditionally, they preferred the conservation of existing values rather than the unpredictability of change. This approach was sustained until Peel challenged the party in 1835 to adopt more pragmatic and realistic policies, ones which would be relevant to a rapidly industrialising society. As Britain experienced the transition to capitalism, the protection of landed and agricultural interests became increasingly irrelevant. This important shift in attitude was further precipitated by the reforms of 1867, 1884 and 1885. The Conservatives had to develop a party which could respond to a mass electorate in order to guarantee their political survival. The modern Conservative Party evolved into a broad-based organisation because it recognised that the party had to be an agent of the current age. It may have retained its traditional support amongst the wealthy, but land is no longer the dominating factor in determining Conservative support. Middle England - that solid group of middle-class professionals and business men - had been converted largely by the end of the nineteenth century, and by the twentieth century working-class support was undoubtedly a consistent factor in the Conservative vote. In this respect, the Conservatives no longer opposed democracy but viewed it as a necessary fact of political life.

The Whigs and Liberals had the advantage of drawing support

from a broader electorate, but they, too, had to adapt to new influences. The middle classes were assimilated more rapidly by the Whigs and Liberals, but this in turn hindered further adjustments. The doctrines of *laissez-faire* capitalism and the freedom of the individual were so fundamental to liberalism by the second half of the nineteenth century that liberalism struggled to establish a coherent response to the needs of a mass electorate. Their efforts, in the shape of New Liberalism, were not sufficient to avert the rise of a working-class party.

The emergence of the Labour Party can be regarded as one of the most significant features of the modern political system. The radical platforms of the French revolutionary era, the Luddites, and the Chartists ended in failure because the ruling classes failed to recognise their legitimate interests. The attitudes of those who ruled were sustained by two beliefs: that those without property should be not be enfranchised and that their interests were nevertheless protected by MPs, despite their narrow base of authority. Once it was accepted that there had to be greater accountability between constituents and their representatives, then it became feasible to contemplate the creation of a party which would cater for working-class interests. The vote empowered the working classes to challenge and reform Britain's political system in a way which would have been inconceivable 100 years earlier. Thus Labour, as the party of the working classes, would succeed whereas earlier groups had failed.

2 How did Britain become a Parliamentary Democracy?

The growth of democracy in Britain was shaped by a range of inter-relating factors: overseas developments, philosophical ideas, economic progress, the impact of greater educational opportunities, as well as the changing expectations of women and labour. In isolation, each factor was not sufficiently powerful to affect long-term political change, but their combined effects were to influence dramatically the distinctive pattern of developing democracy in Britain.

How might each causal factor now be analysed? To what extent, for example, were external events crucial in providing momentum to political reform in Britain? Both the American and French Revolutions illustrated the deficiencies and limitations of parliamentary democracy in Britain. These events facilitated political discussion and inspired political reformers, yet ultimately did they play a key role in determining political change in Britain, especially as their immediate effect was to provoke and strengthen the forces of reaction? It is in this context that it is important to understand the effect of long-term influences. It may not be possible to attribute major political events to the impact of external pressures, but their relevance in terms of affecting a climate of opinion over a period of time does need to be appreciated. Likewise, what was the correlation, if any, between those revolutions and changing political ideas within Britain? Political ideas evolved which gave an ideological framework for British politics. Faced with a choice of extremism or moderation, these ideas rejected the revolutionary solution, but were they any better for promoting a system which prolonged the dominance of the upper and middle classes and excluded the working classes and women? Moreover, if a set of ideas prevailed which provided a logical justification for the extension of the franchise, why was British democracy still so much the product of chance?

It was perhaps this haphazard, almost accidental methodology of granting political concessions which explains why British democracy followed a different pattern from that of revolutionary Europe. The concern to preserve past values rather than to embrace the untested views of radicalism underpinned each step in the reform process. Radical change was also avoided because of the lack of doctrinal ideas and Marxism. Therefore politicians could afford to grant minimal reform, safeguarded by the knowledge that a serious challenge to their authority was unlikely. It was also convenient to portray radicalism as a dangerous threat to the constitution. It provided a neat justification for the exclusion of the undesirable, uneducated masses.

Was the Industrial Revolution a positive or negative factor in helping to determine the growth of democracy in Britain? It could be argued that Britain's role as a leading industrial nation was testimony to the successful partnership of employers and employees which characterised Britain's industrialisation. As a result, the authority and respectability of the middle classes was consolidated and enabled them to become key components in British democracy. A more critical analysis might be appropriate, however. Was it not the case that economic success bred complacency? Why did the political rights of the lower strata of society seem so immaterial unless it was convenient to prolong their role as a subservient group, unable to question the economic superiority of their masters?

This analysis, if valid, also raises the pertinent issue of the rationale behind educational policies. Clearly, one objective was to 'manage' the effects of democracy, yet was it not short-sighted of politicians to assume that a more literate working class would still refrain from questioning their inferior position in society? The long-term effects of increasing educational opportunities were crucial, not only for their role in raising working-class expectations but also in facilitating political change for women. Their enfranchisement was the final strand in the democratic process. As with the working classes, it is important to evaluate whether their enfranchisement was an after-effect, a natural consequence of other, more critical factors.

Ultimately all these ingredients played significant but interconnecting roles in causing the growth of democracy in Britain. There is no simple answer to why Britain acquired her particular strand of democracy, but by understanding and questioning the relative merits of different causal factors, it is possible to attain some appreciation of Britain's democratic system.

3 The Strengths of British Democracy

Britain's democracy was not born out of conflict, war or revolution but evolved over centuries to produce what has often been considered to be a stable and highly respected democracy. Has this gradual process of political change been particularly advantageous?

One element of the evolutionary nature of democracy has been the successful mixture of continuity with the past combined with judicious reform. The composition of Britain's parliamentary institutions has altered in that they became, in the Commons at least, more representative of the people. However, modernisation of the representative system has taken place without the institutions themselves being undermined. The balance of power has certainly shifted so that the sovereignty of Parliament was secured, but this was achieved through consensus tempered by periodic crises. Even though major reforms such as the 1832 Reform Act and the 1911 Parliament Act were associated with constitutional crises, they were nevertheless resolved through normal parliamentary procedures. Despite its unwritten form, it could be argued that the flexibility of the British constitution has been its strength, enabling it to preserve the best features of parliamentary democracy and to withstand potential harm.

The stability of Britain's parliamentary institutions has also been enhanced by a consensus approach to politics. Although leading politicians such as Gladstone and Disraeli were often arch protagonists, engaging in bitter debates, their confrontations were regarded as part of the format of daily political life. They never believed that resistance to a political opponent should be expressed in any way other than through the normal channels of debate. Differences of opinion were tolerated as part of the essential components of democratic government. Despite the adversarial nature of such debates, one of the distinctive aspects of politics in the nineteenth and twentieth centuries was the extent of broad agreement on issues. Both major political parties instigated political reform, undertook social reform and involved the country in foreign wars. Threats to national security have prompted concerted action not division, as exemplified by the coalition governments during the First and Second World Wars.

Another contributory factor to the evolutionary nature of British democracy has been the adaptability of the monarchy. In the eighteenth century, the main constitutional issue was to restrain the monarchy. Reformers deplored the lack of accountability by the Crown to Parliament and feared the growth of absolute monarchy. The abuse of power by the French monarchy gave further incentive to impose limits on the authority of the British Crown. Although there continued to be advocates of republicanism throughout the nineteenth and twentieth centuries, the fact that the monarchy was prepared to relinquish authority to the point where it retained merely symbolic powers proved a positive factor for parliamentary democracy. The sovereignty of Parliament was not threatened. The British monarchy thus avoided the fate of European monarchs who, discredited by their adherence to traditional authority, found themselves in conflict with progressive politics.

Finally, Britain's democracy remained secure because there was a stable relationship between different social classes. This is not to deny that there were and continued to be areas of conflict. From 1780 to 1848, for instance, successive governments had to contend with frequent, violent political radical protests. The coercive powers of the State were applied without compunction. The suppression of the Chartists was perceived as an essential prerequisite to maintaining law and order. The denial of political rights was immaterial. Nevertheless, by the mid-nineteenth century, the disenfranchised saw some merit in working within the capitalist system, not opposing it. The economic incentives arising from the Industrial Revolution encouraged working-class aspirations. Thus the working class sought respectability and enhanced social status and rejected confrontation with the owners of capitalism. One of the reasons that enabled Britain to avoid revolution was because, despite continuing class divisions, potential conflict was suppressed by the traditions of deference and paternalism which promoted cooperation. Probably the most serious event to precipitate class differences and long-term social change was the First World War. Most notably, it was then followed by the first major political reform for over 30 years: the 1918 Parliament Act.

4 Vestiges of the Past or Pillars of Respectability?

The features of democracy discussed above may have served Britain well, but a number of questions remain regarding their place in a modern democracy. Are the relics of the past still relevant or is it now difficult to defend institutions that are overwhelmingly undemocratic?

a) Should Britain have a democratic Second Chamber?

One of the issues highlighted by critics of Britain's constitution is the anomalous position of the House of Lords. In theory, its function should be to provide a constitutional check on the encroachment and abuse of power by the Commons. But this responsibility has fallen into disrepute. The House of Lords can only operate as a legitimate restraining influence if it possesses democratic authority.

In February 1997, there were 616 hereditary peers eligible to sit in the Lords out of a total of 1,058 (58 per cent).[1] Current proposals focus on removing the hereditary peers from the House of Lords, but it is debatable as to whether this alone would make the Lords any more democratic. Is there any merit in retaining the life peers when so many of them are regarded as political appointees, rewarded in the honours system for political service? Should the current House of Lords be replaced by an entirely elected chamber? A more drastic alternative would be to abolish the second chamber entirely, on the grounds that if the Commons is truly democratic, a second chamber should be redundant. Despite the obstacles to abolishing centuries of tradition, there is now an imperative need to reform the House of Lords. As the recent research paper on House of Lords reform admitted:

1   the worst upshot would be if reform of the House of Lords were to lead to years of constitutional tinkering and uncertainty, or if we were to exchange the present House for one which was more rational but less effective. There is a danger in piecemeal change which would alter
5   the balance and nature of the present House without first determining that whatever replaced the existing composition would be as - or more - effective in fulfilling the varied roles of the Second Chamber.[2]

b) Monarchy or Republic?

The other vestige of the past is the monarchy. The monarchy's constitutional role is largely ceremonial, and many critics assert that its remaining responsibilities are obscured by the mystique surrounding the institution. In addition, the members of the royal family are perceived to be too remote from their subjects. Does such an institution, which is so totally undemocratic in terms of derivation of authority, still hold a valid place in a modern democracy?

Supporters consider that there is a future role for the monarchy. A constitutional monarchy can provide stability and continuity amidst political change. If the monarchy were to modernise itself by abandoning the trappings of ceremony, then maybe the institution would seem less isolated from normal civilian life. Shirley Williams, founder member of the Social Democratic Party, argued in 1994 that the monarchy could redeem itself by becoming a 'citizen monarch',[3] bringing it more in line with the style of monarchy seen in Denmark and Belgium. At the very least, there exists now a strong tide of opinion which would endorse a more personable, slimmed-down version of the monarchy.

The stark alternative would be to reject centuries of tradition, abolish the monarchy and become a republic. But is it appropriate to have a head of state beholden to any political party? Would Britain want to emulate the American style of politics, for example, where a president representing the Democratic Party has to work with a Congress, America's equivalent of the British Parliament, dominated by the Republicans? In addition, an American president seeking re-election can spend the second half of his first four-year term of office concentrating more on how to secure a second term of office than on judicious government. There may indeed be ways of avoiding such partisan politics. The head of state could be non-political, leaving our parliamentary government to function relatively unchanged. The criteria for selecting such candidates would pose an interesting question for all students of politics.

5 An Imperfect Democracy?

In addition to the idiosyncratic presence of undemocratic institutions in a supposed democracy, other features of our current political system beg the question of whether further reform is now essential. Have we become too complacent about the merits of our constitution to the extent that we overlook its many faults? Those urging constitutional reform decry the unfairness of the electoral system, the huge executive powers wielded by a government elected by a minority, and the consequent demise of Parliament's sovereignty, as well as the frequent undermining of individual liberties. Criticism is also voiced against the manipulation of information, especially by the media, which results in an ill-informed electorate. These weaknesses are partly attributable to the absence of a written constitution. As a result, there are often unclear boundaries regarding what is legitimate government action. How could the British political system be reformed and would a more perfect democracy ever be feasible?

a) The Case for Proportional Representation

One popular criticism of British politics is that we depend on the first-past-the-post system to select our MPs (see page 2). Victory at a national level goes to the party with the highest number of seats although it is possible for a majority government to possess fewer votes than the opposition. This system is favoured because it generally produces strong, stable government. The electorate selects from two major parties, one to rule, the other to oppose, whilst small, extremist parties are prevented from acquiring any political influence. Despite the rise of the Liberal Democrats since 1979, at the 1997 general election most voters knew that they had only two possible political choices for the next government.

What did this election result produce? Examine the statistics in the table on page 128:[4]

Distribution of seats and votes in the 1997 UK general election		
	% votes	% seats	Total number of seats
Labour	43.3	63.6	419
Conservative	30.7	25.0	165
Lib. Dem.	16.8	7.0	46

The Labour Party's landslide victory overturned 18 years of consistent Conservative rule. But can Labour, or any previous government, claim to have a mandate to represent the people when the composition of the legislature is not in proportion with the distribution of the popular vote? This questionable method of selecting a government is further compounded by the effects of the first-past-the-post system in individual constituencies. Even in a three-way fight, a candidate can win with only 40 per cent of the votes, leaving 60 per cent, the majority, without a representative of their interests. This makes a mockery of the notion that democracy means rule by the majority.

What are the alternatives? The obvious choice is some form of Proportional Representation (PR) in which the allocation of seats would more accurately reflect the corresponding percentage of votes cast. Unfortunately, there are a range of PR systems, all with their relative strengths and weaknesses. One proposal, the Alternative Vote, would retain single member constituencies, giving voters the opportunity to state their first, second and third preferences from a list of candidates. Assume there are three candidates. If, on the first count, no candidate achieved 50 per cent of the votes cast, the last candidate would be eliminated from the list. Votes cast for this candidate would then be redistributed according to the second preferences of his voters. Redistribution of votes would continue until one candidate emerged with an absolute majority. Arguably, this would result in fairer representation in the Commons, with smaller parties like the Liberal Democrats benefiting most.

However, what would be the costs of such a system? Consider the possible outcome. Instead of a majority government, albeit elected on a minority of votes, there would probably be several parties in Parliament, none with an overall majority. Each would have to bargain for power, no doubt seeking a coalition with an acceptable bedfellow. This could be an advantage. What is wrong with negotiation and compromise, with agreement rather than adversarial politics? A coalition based on consensus could be far more productive than one party in power forever seeking to score points against the opposition. But traditions die hard in Britain, and it is questionable whether either of the two main parties would ever sacrifice their current political advantage for the sake of more representative politics.

b) A Written Constitution

Britain's unwritten constitution has traditionally been defended on the grounds that its flexibility has permitted prudent reforms and adjustments. In theory, its strengths were that it established a system of checks and balances which purported to uphold parliamentary sovereignty and which produced a stable democracy. This in turn served as a model for democracies elsewhere.

Critics dispute the merits of the British constitution. Whilst Britain's reputation may have rested on a perception of secure democracy, her democracy itself was never enshrined in written laws. The rules and principles which came to be embodied in the British constitution evolved through a mixture of custom and legal practice over centuries. The problem with such a haphazard method of defining a constitution was that it could so easily be undermined by governments because they were not beholden to any clearly defined rules. In contrast, other countries sought to embody their principles of democratic government in laws: a written constitution.

Those seeking to modernise Britain's democracy argue that her constitution is in desperate need of reform. Parliament's sovereignty has become a facade due to encroachment by a powerful executive, namely the Cabinet. Given the imprecise nature of the constitution, there are no formal means of holding a government accountable for its actions except at the next general election. Governments with large majorities can ride roughshod over the views of the Commons, even their own party members, whilst Cabinet ministers can effectively make policy decisions without any proper scrutiny. Some prime ministers can almost ignore their Cabinets.

Should Britain now halt this insidious accumulation of central powers by governments and adopt a written constitution? Supporters argue that this would specify in law the relationship between the government and the people, defining the powers of the executive, the legislature and the judiciary. It would also assist the restoration of local democracy which is widely felt to have been harmed by centralisation of government. With appropriate protection in law, reformers assert that Britain would finally achieve a more truly democratic government.

c) A Bill of Rights

Correlated to the need for a written constitution is the belief that Parliament and the legal system do not adequately protect individual rights and liberties. No minimum standard concerning basic human rights exists, with the result that the right to free speech, assembly or right to a fair trial are not prescribed by law. These rights are considered fundamental to democracy, yet they can be infringed in Britain by governments anxious, for example, to protect national security.

What would be the purpose of a Bill of Rights? Given that many individuals in Britain have had to resort to the European Court of Human Rights in order to challenge decisions made in Britain, there would appear to be a strong argument in favour of enforcing individual rights by law in Britain. Defining those rights would be a challenge. Individual liberty has to be accommodated alongside the need to protect others from danger and violence. Likewise, should language which incites people to riot and threaten other people's safety be permitted? Many people argue, however, that at the very least Britain should adopt the European Convention on Human Rights into British law.

d) An Open and Informed Democracy?

To what extent is the public properly informed? Critics assert that democracy is impeded by an inability to make informed choices caused by government secrecy and the media's control of information. Public access to information can be widely restricted, the Official Secrets Act being just one example of government control. Following the revelations in 1987 about contaminated beef in Britain, much controversy arose about whether the public had been kept fully briefed on possible dangers to their health. With computer technology advancing so rapidly, the potential for abusing access to information is enormous. Should the government now implement a Freedom of Information Act to provide the necessary protection?

Another area of concern is the role of the media. To what extent does the media manipulate information? The press is frequently guilty of publishing prejudiced information, a most notable example being the *Sun's* election headline on 9 April 1992, exhorting its readers of dire consequences if they voted for Neil Kinnock and the Labour Party: 'If Kinnock wins today will the last person to leave Britain please turn out the lights'.[5] Coverage of elections often seems to highlight personalities rather than policies. Given a choice between reporting a keynote speech on policy or a negative attack by one politician against another, the latter approach will often prevail. Britain has not yet witnessed the kind of character defamation in television advertisements which accompanies much of the electioneering practices in America because current libel laws prevent this. But with every election we seem to come closer to losing a balanced portrayal of the issues for the sake of glitzy presentation. The implications for the electorate are that they end up voting without being able to make informed choices. The dilemma is whether we retain our functional parliamentary democracy, or permit greater freedom, in which case the manipulation of information might be an unwelcome outcome.

6 Conclusion: The Future of Democracy in Britain

No single country has developed an impeccable democratic government. When America and France fought for democracy in the late eighteenth century, the result was far from perfect. Even today neither they, nor any other country, can claim to possess a faultless system of democracy. Even if democracy is enshrined in a written constitution, it is often distorted in practice. The potential threats to democracy are numerous. Corruption pervades many countries, as do social and economic inequality. Racial and religious minorities are often forced into the position of second-class citizens, despite the supposed protection of democratic government.

So what does the future hold for Britain? Although we have many imperfections, one conclusion might be that change must not be undertaken lightly. Our political institutions have survived the test of history, provided security and stability in the face of war and revolutions, and resisted both communism and fascism. Over time, our democracy has evolved and modernised itself to reflect the changes and expectations of a modern age. Despite its many faults, parliamentary government in conjunction with a constitutional monarchy has demonstrated several strengths. Likewise, local government has continued to provide an essential channel for the implementation of democracy at the grass-roots.

Yet change cannot be avoided. As the values of society change, so practices that were tolerated 20 years ago become unacceptable. Inequality persists in many forms, the inevitable consequence of living in a capitalist society where economic freedom is so highly valued. But if the past is anything to go by, the future remains uncertain and unpredictable. Political theory will be diluted by practical realities and the outcome will continue to be an imperfect compromise. In the end, this may suffice.

References

1   *House of Lords 'Reform': Recent Proposals*, Research Paper 97/28 (House of Commons Library, February 1997), p.30.
2   Ibid, p.27.
3   Shirley Williams, 'A Citizen Monarchy', in Anthony Barnett (ed), *Power and the Throne. The Monarchy Debate* (Vintage in association with Charter 88, 1994), p.63.
4   Pippa Norris, 'Anatomy of a Labour Landslide', in Pippa Norris and Neil T. Gavin, (eds), *Britain Votes 1997* (Oxford University Press, 1997), p.2.
5   *Sun*, 9 April 1992.

Chronological Table

1688		Revolution Settlement
1689		Bill of Rights
1760		George III became king
1776	4 July	American Declaration of Independence
		Publication of Adam Smith's *An Inquiry into the Nature and Causes of the Wealth of Nations*
1780		Westminster Association issued a six-point programme of reform
1785		Pitt's proposals for parliamentary reform defeated
1787		Federal Constitution of the United States adopted
1789	9 July	Constituent Assembly in France established
	14 July	Storming of the Bastille, Paris
1790		Publication of Burke's *Reflections on the Revolution in France*
1791		Publication of Paine's *Rights of Man*, Part I
1792	Jan	London Corresponding Society founded
	Feb	Publication of *Rights of Man*, Part II
		Publication of Mary Wollstonecraft's *Vindication of the Rights of Women*
	Sept	French Republic declared
1793	Jan	Execution of Louis XVI
1795		Treasonable Practices Act and Seditious Meetings Act passed
1799-1800		Combination Acts prevented trade unions
1806	Jan	Death of William Pitt
1811		Start of Luddite protests
1815	20 Nov	Treaty of Paris - end of wars with France
1816	Dec	Spa Field demonstrations for parliamentary reform
1819	16 Aug	'Peterloo Massacre', St. Peter's Fields, Manchester
	Dec	Six Acts passed, introducing tough legislation to suppress radicalism
1820	Jan	Death of George III; succeeded by George IV
1824		Repeal of Combination Acts of 1799 and 1800
1827	Feb	The Prime Minister, Lord Liverpool, resigned due to a stroke
1828	Jan	Wellington became Prime Minister
	May	Test and Corporation Acts repealed granting civil rights to Dissenters
1829	April	Catholic Emancipation Act gave civil rights to Catholics
1830	June	Death of George IV; his brother, William IV, became king

	June-Aug	'Swing Riots': agricultural protests
	Nov	Wellington resigned as Prime Minister; succeeded by Lord Grey, leader of the Whigs
1831	1 Mar	Introduction of First Reform Bill in the Commons
	April	Bill defeated; general election held
	July	Second Reform Bill introduced
	Oct	Bill defeated in House of Lords, followed by widespread riots
1832	Mar	Third Reform Bill passed by Commons
	May	Defeated in the Lords; Grey resigned Wellington failed to form a government Grey returned as PM
	June	Lords passed Reform Bill
1834		Poor Law Amendment Act set up workhouses for the destitute
1835		Publication of Peel's Tamworth Manifesto Municipal Corporations Act established elected local councils
1837	June	Death of William IV; accession of Queen Victoria
1838	May	Publication of the 'People's Charter' with six-point programme of political reform
1848		Revolutions in Europe Third Chartist petition rejected; collapse of the Chartist movement
1859		Emergence of the Liberal Party
1864		Reform Union founded
1865		Death of Lord Palmerston Reform League founded
1866		Introduction of Reform Bill to Commons by Lord Russell and William Gladstone
	June	Bill defeated, Liberals resigned New government led by Lord Derby and Disraeli
1867	Mar	Disraeli introduced new Reform Bill
	Aug	Second Reform Act passed after many amendments
1869		Municipal Franchise Act: single women ratepayers could vote in local elections
1870		Forster's Education Act established elementary schools funded by ratepayers
1872		Ballot Act, introduced the secret ballot
1883		Corrupt and Illegal Practices (Prevention) Act
1884		Third Reform Act
1885		Redistribution of Seats Act
1888		Local Government Act established County Councils
1893	Jan	Founding of Independent Labour Party - Bradford

1897		National Union of Women's Suffrage founded
1900		Labour Representation Committee founded
1901		Death of Queen Victoria; succeeded by Edward VII
1903		Women's Social and Political Union founded
1909	April	The 'People's Budget'
1910	6 May	Death of Edward VII; succeeded by George V
1911	10 Aug	Parliament Act passed by House of Lords, limiting Lords' veto
1918		Representation of the People Act (Fourth Reform Act)
1928		Equal Franchise Act, granted votes to men and women aged 21
1948		Representation of the People Act
1969		Representation of the People Act, lowered voting age to 18

Further Reading

There are a wide range of books on British political history but few provide a thematic study of democracy in Britain. The best approach is to gain a broad understanding of the period by studying some general books, then read some more detailed analysis of individual political parties, philosophical ideas, and social and economic trends.

1 General Books

A useful starting point is Michael Bentley, *Politics Without Democracy, 1815-1914*, 2nd edn (Fontana, 1996), which examines the transition to democracy in Britain and in particular looks at the role of Britain's governing classes. Additional insights can be gained from D.G. Wright, *Democracy and Reform, 1815-1885* (Longman, 1970), which analyses the peaceful process of democratic change in Britain. One of the few books to discuss the end of the eighteenth century is Eric J. Evans, *Political Parties in Britain 1783-1867* (Methuen, 1985). This gives a succinct, manageable introduction to the British political system and the emergence of a modern party system. In contrast, R. Stewart, *Party and Politics, 1830-1852* (Macmillan, 1989) has a more narrow focus, but one which is equally important. Martin Pugh, *The Making of Modern British Politics, 1867-1939*, 2nd edn (Blackwell, 1993) is essential reading, not least for its challenging and provocative analysis of political, social and economic developments. For an understanding of politics at the time of George III, J. Brewer, *Party, Ideology and Popular Politics at the Accession of George III* (CUP, 1976) is immensely useful. J. Belchem, *Class, Party and the Political System in Britain, 1867-1914* (Blackwell, 1990) gives a very valuable study into the way 'class' politics had an impact on the process of democratisation. Finally, there are a number of *Access to History* books which can be read in conjunction with *The Growth of Democracy in Britain*. Of these, Robert Pearce and Roger Stearn, *Government and Reform 1815-1918* (Hodder & Stoughton, 1994) contains a very useful chapter (Chapter 5) on local government.

2 The Liberal Party

R. Douglas, *A History of the Liberal Party* (Macmillan, 1976) gives a good, if somewhat pro-Liberal interpretation of the history of the Liberal Party. J.R. Vincent's *The Formation of the Liberal Party, 1857-1868* (Constable, 1966) was a major book for its evaluation of the Liberal Party, although its in-depth analysis may deter some readers. Michael Bentley, *The Climax of Liberal Politics, 1868-1918* (Edward Arnold, 1987) contains an important study of the crises facing liberalism during this period. George Dangerfield's *The Strange Death of Liberal England* (Paladin, 1935) is still regarded as a controversial, although now somewhat out-dated, investigation into the causes of the Liberals' collapse. Another key book in the historiographical debate about the decline of the Liberals is P.F. Clarke's *Lancashire and the New Liberalism* (CUP, 1971). In the *Access to History* series, Duncan Watts's *Whigs, Radicals and Liberals 1815-1914* (Hodder & Stoughton, 1995), is a useful, additional reference book.

3 The Conservative Party

Bruce Coleman, *Conservatism and the Conservative Party in the Nineteenth Century* (Edward Arnold, 1987) gives a very authoritative analysis of the development of the Conservative Party from the late eighteenth century to the end of the nineteenth century. A crucial period in the history of the party is dealt with in E.J. Feuchtwanger's *Disraeli, Democracy and the Tory Party* (Clarendon Press, 1968). Issues of Conservative ideology in late Victorian Britain are expertly tackled in Martin Pugh's *The Tories and the People, 1880-1935* (Blackwell, 1985).

See also the *Access to History* volume by Duncan Watts, *Tories, Conservatives and Unionists 1815-1914* (Hodder & Stoughton, 1994).

4 Political Radicalism

An excellent introduction to the history of popular radicalism is D.G. Wright's *Popular Radicalism: the Working-Class Experience, 1780-1880* (Longman, 1991), whilst a shorter, but equally worthwhile book is H.T. Dickinson's *British Radicalism and the French Revolution, 1789-1815* (Blackwell, 1985). E.P. Thompson's *The Making of the English Working Class* (Penguin, 1968) is very detailed, but immensely significant for its interpretation of working-class movements. For a more pragmatic understanding of the nature of the British working class, see E.H. Hunt, *British Labour History, 1815-1914* (Weidenfeld and Nicolson, 1981). Two books join the debate about the rise of the Labour Party and the subsequent decline of the Liberals: K. Laybourn, *The Rise of Labour: The British Labour Party 1890-1979* (Edward Arnold, 1988) and Ross McKibbin, *The Evolution of the Labour Party, 1910-1924* (OUP, 1974). Both emphasise the level of working-class political activity prior to 1914.

5 Social and Economic

Harold Perkin, *The Origins of Modern English Society, 1780-1880* (Routledge, Kegan and Paul, 1969) gives a very comprehensive analysis of pre-industrial England and its transition to a modern, class-based society. Asa Briggs', *The Age of Improvement 1783-1867* (Longman, 1979) is a classic text, which provides a good mix of social, economic and political history. A more recent and original discussion of the British economy is found in Roderick Floud's *The People and the British Economy, 1830-1914* (OUP, 1997), which concentrates on the relationship between different groups in society and the economic power of Britain.

6 Women's History

Martin Pugh, *Women's Suffrage in Britain, 1867-1928* (Historical Association, 1980) is a very useful, concise examination of the women's suffrage movement and the reasons for gaining the vote. See also Martin Pugh, *Women and the Women's Movement in Britain, 1914-1959* (MacMillan, 1992), especially for its focus on post First World War issues. A more sympathetic analysis can be found in Sandra Stanley Holton's *Feminism and Democracy: Women's Suffrage and Reform Politics in Britain, 1900-1918* (CUP, 1986).

7 Elections

Two books are particularly valuable for their explanations of the electoral system: Martin Pugh, *The Evolution of the British Electoral System, 1832-1987* (Historical Association, 1988) and H.J. Hanham, *Elections and Party Management in the time of Disraeli and Gladstone* (Harvester Press, 1978). The first contains a broad, but concise account of electoral reform, whilst the latter deals with the problems associated with the growth of party organisation after 1867. Specific issues such as proportional representation are tackled in Enid Lakeman's *How Democracies Vote* (Faber and Faber, 1974) and Vernon Bogdanor and David Butler (eds), *Democracy and Elections: Electoral Systems and their Political Consequences* (CUP, 1983).

8 Documents and Sources

A good selection of documents can be found in A. Aspinall and E. Anthony Smith (eds), *English Historical Documents, 1783-1832*, vol.8 (Routledge, 1996), G.M. Young and W.D. Handcock (eds), *English Historical Documents 1833-1874*, vol.9 (Routledge, 1996) and W.D. Handcock (ed), *English Historical Documents 1874-1914*, vol.10 (Routledge, 1996). H.J. Hanham, *The Nineteenth Century Constitution 1815-1914: Documents and Commentary* (CUP, 1969) contains a wide range of documents on constitutional and government issues. K.O. Morgan, *The Age of Lloyd George* (Allen and Unwin, 1978) has valuable documents for the early twentieth century. The writings of key political thinkers are all available: Tom Paine, *The Rights of Man*, edited by Tony Benn (J.M. Dent, 1993); Edmund Burke, *Reflections on the Revolution in France*, edited by Conor Cruise O'Brien (Penguin, 1986); James Mill, *Essays on Government, Jurisprudence, Liberty of the Press, and Law of Nations* (Clarendon Press, 1978); J.S. Mill, *On Liberty and Other Essays*, edited John Gray (OUP, 1998); Walter Bagehot, *The English Constitution* (Fontana, 1993). Finally, a good CD-ROM collection of contemporary newspaper articles can be found in *The Times Perspectives: History in the Making* (News Multimedia Ltd).

Index